THE WORLD HASN'T PROGRESSED IN 5,000 YEARS

Larry Couchmanos

authorHOUSE®

AuthorHouse™
1663 Liberty Drive
Bloomington, IN 47403
www.authorhouse.com
Phone: 1-800-839-8640

First published by AuthorHouse 8/6/2010

ISBN: 978-1-4520-3711-0 (e)
ISBN: 978-1-4520-3710-3 (sc)

Printed in the United States of America

This book is printed on acid-free paper.

TABLE OF CONTENTS

CONVERSATION WITH KOSTA

My favorite thing about this book is that I don't know what I will write about. I have just watched *Dinner with Andre* which I found extremely interesting. Do I believe everything Andre was saying? Absolutely not. Do I think he's wrong in everything he said? Well no, I don't. But that's the point. This is going to branch off to another topic that I was hoping to write about.

The title of this chapter is "Conversations with Kosta." I recently had a breakfast with my brother Kosta where he gave me some advice on life and how I should conduct myself. He also told me what I should focus on. The inherent problem in this is that nobody should tell you these things. They may be able to make suggestions; but, it is my life and I will live it the way I want. Still though, I couldn't help but listen to what he had to say.

I am writing this chapter a week after our conversation. Some would argue that I should have written this when I returned home from our conversation. I disagree because when you write about it a week later, you realize the things you really felt were important because those are the things that stayed with you for a week. Waiting makes you forget all the unimportant things that were said. Now, what is important versus what is unimportant is objective; but, that is not to say that what I consider important is correct. The previous statement is not a typo; I meant to say that what is important is objective. This chapter is serving as an outline for what I actually want to write about in this book.

One thing Kosta mentioned was that I need to stop talking (or in this case writing) as fast as I can think, but, I need to pause. He talked very vehemently about the importance of pausing during a story. As I was watching *Dinner with Andre,* I paid attention to Andre as he talked throughout the dinner and thought of Kosta's theory. Here's a guy who was so interesting to talk to that a movie was written about an hour and half long conversation between he and his friend. Surely, he's a great story teller. However, what I found was, he didn't pause the way Kosta described; but, he told stories the way I tell stories to people with whom I am close. Kosta was reacting to an occasion when I quickly fit in a story to our waiter from Crete. Unlike Kosta, I am not someone who will just spark up a conversation with someone. While my brother and the waiter were talking, Kosta said accurately that I believed this was a conversation between Kosta and the waiter; not the three of us. This is why my story was rushed. I often tell this type of story to my supervisor at work when she's about to leave because that is the only time I feel I should talk to her about personal issues. Knowing that she has to catch a bus to begin her 2.5 hour commute, I must rush the story. The point is, though, I tell the same few stories over and over again and when Kosta was lecturing me on his theory on storytelling, a variety of thoughts swam through my head.

One thing that Kosta said that fascinated me on many levels was, "You have more life experience than everyone sitting in this room."

At the time, we were still sitting at a diner. I looked around instinctively as if I could look at a person and tell where they've been. I failed in this attempt, obviously, but as I thought about it, what he said was extremely insightful yet insanely naïve at the exact same time. This week I've been walking around with a swagger for literally the first time in my life. It's not arrogance; it's the idea that despite my quick tweets about my views on life using a pseudonym, I have few followers (13), the people I associate with have given me feedback that has made me realize I have been stupid for not seeing it for myself. People tell me, "You always have the best stories." Or, when AIM was popular, I would put up an away message of a quotation I found remarkable and many people would respond, "You always have the best quotes." My typical response to the first remark is, "I almost never do anything; but, when I do something, it's a great story!" Now, this may be for a variety of reasons. The most logical explanation is that I refuse to do things just to do something. I almost wrote, "I don't do things for the sake of doing them" but that is completely different. In fact, I do do things for the sake of doing them; I just call it, "doing things for the sentence."

Even the Puerto Rican grandmother at work has told me I should write a book. She even said that if I didn't, she would write a book about our arguments based on my positions. Now, I consider myself a writer so why wouldn't I write this book? David Sedaris' book, *Me Speak Pretty One Day* is insanely popular; yet, all he does is write a couple chapters about completely unrelated experiences in his life. If an uptight little writing purist priss, and there were a number of them at New York University (NYU), is reading this and says they believe I'm mistaken and that the underlying flow of the book was x, I will say you are a fucking moron. To prove my point, I would make copies of each chapter of *Me Speak Pretty One Day* (remember I'm assuming this is a college professor) and give a different chapter to each of his or her students and tell them to read it. When they came back, I would ask them to report on it. Now, don't pay attention to what they actually say, pay attention to the fact that they are able to do the task. The simple fact that they can report on a chapter of *Me Speak Pretty One Day* without any knowledge of the other chapters in the book proves that you are indeed wrong for believing that the book flows. It is a collection of short stories of different experiences in Sedaris' life and his take on them. Despite its simplicity, the book is insanely successful. So why can't I do the same thing?

What was really naïve about what Kosta said was that he doesn't seem to realize that he was in the room too. He even said to me, "I'm jealous of the things you've done."

When I do challenge his views, which I hope to get into later, he merely says, "Well, you're 25, you don't know what you're talking about." Or simply, "Trust me, I'm right about this." This is coming from a mathematical, scientific mind like his. This, however, doesn't make him logical because logical minds and mathematical, scientific minds are very different. If you don't believe me, then notice that lawyers or people studying for the LSAT do not have mathematical or scientific minds. In fact, the LSAT reading comprehension selections are often about science because the test writers know the people taking the test don't have scientific minds and aren't very interested in science. Therefore, the section tests how well individuals do at reading a segment and answering related questions regarding a topic in which they have no interest. My response to Kosta should have been, "I should lecture you about life because I am actually living life, whereas you are not."

Now does that mean I don't have any respect for what he said?

Absolutely not. I have remarkable respect for Kosta because he's one of the smartest people I have ever known, but, he is unable to see simplicity because he believes that nothing can be simple. Despite his mathematical mind, he was unable to figure out the pattern below. See if you can figure out the next sequence in this pattern.

1
11
21
1211
111221

Also, when I gave him the riddle, "A girl's mother dies, at the funeral she meets a guy who she becomes completely enamored with, but, she forgets to give him her contact information or any way of getting a hold of her. She then kills her sister. Why did she kill her sister?"

Unfortunately, I will never know whether I would get this answer correct. Almost every person I have ever asked has gotten it relatively quickly. At first, I was asking people whom I believe may have homicidal tendencies. The reason I was asking people who have homicidal tendencies is because the question isn't really a riddle. It is used by psychologists to determine if someone is a sociopath. If you get it right, then it shows evidence (psychologists never use the word 'prove') that you are capable of mass murder and may become a serial killer. I have purposely devoted much time between the riddle and the answer because I want you, the reader, to stop reading and think about it. When I read the riddle in a book; I kept reading and got to the answer in the next line without ever thinking about it. I asked Kosta to test a different theory since I know Kosta is not capable of being a serial killer. To the psychologists point, when I told someone who went to law school (well, he dropped out after a year), he couldn't get the answer and he is extremely logical. Take that as you will. Well, if you refused to think about it or have thought about it but can't figure it out, I guess that's a good thing. Kosta is the only person to respond this way though, "It can't be that she wanted there to be another funeral so she could see the guy again because that's too easy."

This is a very intriguing answer because A) that is the correct answer and B) Why is it that if something is easy, it can't be right? Obviously, Kosta has this belief. Now, I think if you get this question quickly it shows your ability to divorce emotions and solve the problem. Thinking without emotion is precisely how one should think. Western society is based on this concept. You are wrong if you think emotions help in coming up with a correct answer. Objectivity doesn't deal with emotions and I try not to either. My being human stops me from this. How complicated would your life be if you were to dismiss everything simply because it was too simple? Based on his answer, Kosta is incapable of realizing and enjoying the simple things in life, and that is really sad.

Now, although I wanted to devote an entire chapter to this, the comment, "You're 25, you have no idea what you're talking about" is both absurd and true. The absurd thing, to go against my belief that all things are objective, is that Kosta said it. He is 29. A 29-year-old has no business saying this to a 25-year-old. Also, chronological age is meaningless since life experiences are what's important. The interesting thing is that Kosta has admitted that I have more life experience than he does; but, even if you don't believe that, he is only four years older than I am. This isn't the four years between sophomore year of college and one year removed from college. This is four years between 25 and 29, where, in most cases, and definitely in Kosta's case, not much has happened. All that has happened to Kosta between 25 and 29 is he has continued to fail in trying to promote and expand my dad's company, thinking that he's learning; yet, in reality, he makes the same mistakes over and over again, trusts the wrong people, and has absolutely the worst judge of character I have ever seen.

He tried telling me during our breakfast together that he is a great judge of character and can tell someone's personality within the first five minutes of meeting him or her. I couldn't help but laugh out loud and told him that he was wrong. Everything else he said had potential wisdom in it except that statement. I do have that ability and when determining whether or not to be friends with someone based on the first five minutes of our first encounter, I have only been wrong twice. I have met a lot of people throughout my life, and that is an amazing success rate. If you're curious, I'm 1-1 in that one person I thought was a good person to be friends with turned out not to be and I cut ties with him and the other person who I didn't want to speak to ever again is now one of my closest friends. I have accurately identified everyone else as friend or not. I'm actually quite proud of that. Unfortunately for Kosta, this is not something you learn or can be taught (not sure of the difference in something that can't be learned and something that can't be taught, but I repeat it for emphasis or in case you mistakenly believe there is a difference.)

Just so you don't stop reading because I may come off as arrogant, I say, "You're wrong," to encourage you not to just mindlessly read but to think about the things I say and argue with me. Now, you will get no feedback from me because I'm not sitting with you, but, by arguing with the words, you will be arguing with yourself to see if you agree or disagree What I pray you don't believe is that it depends on the person or that it is just my opinion. You're missing the point. Of course it's my opinion and it doesn't depend on the person, opinions on any topic have a right and a wrong answer. Almost none of my friends agree with almost anything I say; but, the one thing we do agree on when arguing is that one of us is right and one is wrong. This is what cements the friendship. People who don't believe this end up hating me eventually and really, I don't know who they were kidding when they tried to be friends with someone like me in the first place. If you say, "Who are you to say this?" or "I'm arrogant" I will answer "I'm a human being just like you and I'm speaking on what I have learned through my 25 years of experience. I'm not arrogant, I normally am very pessimistic, especially about myself and who I am."

We are all flawed; but, I strive to know the objective truth regarding a topic and so should you. There will be more on this belief later.

Let's go back to my conversation with Kosta. He really can't respond, "You're 25, you have no idea what you're talking about."

When my supervisor, the Puerto Rican grandmother, my parents and others of similar age say the same thing, I feel they have *some* merit in saying this, but not really. Kosta has absolutely no merit in saying this because he has never done anything remotely similar to what I've done and he is less than five years older than I am. So, even if chronological age means something, it is still meaningless for him to say this comment to me. And the whole "Trust me, I'm right," is an indication that I have won the argument in my 10 second rebuttal to his 15 minute speech because for someone as intelligent as Kosta to respond in that way with no evidence or justification means my point stands strong. Just for the record, I feel the same way when someone answers, "You're 25; you have no idea what you're talking about."

Another thing Kosta was saying comes in the form of his complimenting me. He said the difference between a man and a boy is that a man can say more by saying less. This goes to my previous point that my 10 second response completely disarmed his argument to the point that he had to resort to an idiotic statement like "Trust me, I'm right about this." This has no intrinsic point whatsoever and he just admitted that my rebuttal succeeded in disarming him of his point because he couldn't think of a way to respond. He told me that he is already seeing that I talk slower and say more with fewer words. Now as I belittle Kosta by disarming his 15 minute speech with a 10 second response, it still doesn't take away from the fact that he has a point when he gives his definition of the difference between a boy and a man. Plato even remarked on this when he said, "A wise person speaks because he has something to say, a foolish person speaks because he has to say something."

Whether you agree with Plato or not, if you have ever been around a little kid, you can immediately see this point. I hate children, but I have spent a lot of time with little kids, whether it's my cousins, (both my parents are the eldest in their families so I'm older than all my first cousins despite being the third child), friends' nieces or siblings, my godparents' kids or whatever the case may be, I find that despite my hatred for little kids, I am in their company very often. This is why I'm confident you see my point as well. My question to you now is, how many times have you heard a little kid say, "Guess what?" followed by a story that they told with a lot of excitement and enjoyment thinking it was the greatest story in the world? The child also told it at a speed that, despite your fluency in the language they're speaking, was difficult to grasp, and you responded with, "Okay," "That's nice" or some derivation of that. Now, how many times have you spoken to an adult and had the same experience? I immediately thought of this and realized that my brother's definition is sound based on that little test. I asked him what it is that I said that prompted him to say this to me and he didn't remember, which, he says, proves his point. I agree, if I told a story that you don't remember shortly after hearing it, then, I probably did come across like a little kid because I never remember anything a youngster tells me, even shortly after he or she tells a story because of the extreme speed with which he or she tells it. Can you remember the substance of any story a little kid has told you starting with, "Guess what?" If you can't, think about the cognitive dissonance you should have had when I first brought it up and now that you can't remember an example. The solution to the cognitive dissonance is that Kosta is right; you don't listen to a story told like a little kid at great speeds. If you have a better explanation, I wish I were there to hear it.

Another part of my conversation with Kosta that fascinated me was how he failed to see himself in his criticism of others. The basic point of people accusing others of things they're guilty of has always fascinated me. I see this very often because I'm amused by the fact that my friends, who don't get along with one another, almost always have the same comments to say about each other. Now, in order for the point to be true, both parties have to be correct in their criticism of the other; and, for the most part, that is a true statement; but, it's still amusing to hear.

I remarked to Kosta how almost everywhere I turn, people talk badly about him. When I told Kosta what people have been saying about him, he reacted how I expected him to at first, with little emotion. One of the reasons I like talking to Kosta is because he can speak on topics and not bring emotion into it. The key words in my interpretation of Kosta's response to the harsh criticisms by my family, people I grew up with, my friends, and almost everyone who has ever met Kosta is "at first." We were on this topic before breakfast when I spoke with him from about 2:30AM till 6:30AM. We then had breakfast, had a conversation, and then he drove me to the airport. In the car to the airport, all of a sudden Kosta became enraged. During our first 2:30AM – 6:30AM conversation, he said he was bothered by the fact that these people would tell his brother all these negative things about him, thinking it wouldn't get back to him. I do keep secrets, but absolutely none of them ever said not to tell Kosta; and, to be honest, they should expect me to tell him. After all, he is my brother. It baffled me though that hours later, he was still enraged. In the 25 years I have known Kosta, I can't recall one other situation in which something made him mad, then he diverted to other topics, and then went back to discussing what he was mad about hours later. I said as much and he just went back to trying to write off how he wasn't bothered but clearly he was. He gave a couple quick reasons why this instance was different and then he got back to his rant. I had mentioned a number of close family friends who had insulted him, then he went after all of them with unfair comments that I will not discuss specifically because he asked me not to. The two comments that were consistent through all of his attacks were that they still lived in Cleveland and that they worked for their fathers.

Kosta's rant against our family friends was absolutely amazing for me to see. Mostly because of how naïve it is, but also because it gives some insight into how Kosta values things. First off, aside from creating extremely complex computer systems for my families' companies, Kosta has never made anything of himself on his own. Despite being educated at a highly reputable university, he has no idea what it's like to go on a job interview or to search for a job. He has worked with my dad for his entire working career and has failed in every business venture that he has tried, including driving my fathers companies to the ground. In fact, the problem with my family business is that Kosta worked *with* my dad and not *for* my dad. If Kosta had actually worked for my father, maybe my family wouldn't have had the financial difficulties they have had. Kosta couldn't even use my father's success as a crutch to help him be successful because he just drove the whole thing and his opportunity to the ground. I hear that 90% of businesses fail when the father is successful and he passes the business onto his son. Kosta and my father are no exception.

Before I begin this, I should point out, in case you don't know me that I grew up in Cleveland, Ohio. I do feel sorry for people who have never left Cleveland. It's a horrible place to live if you don't have a family. It's a great place to raise children, but, given that I don't want to do that, I have no business in Cleveland. When I'm in Cleveland, I lash out. I'm immediately depressed and if I ever live there again, the only thing that would stop me from committing suicide is fear of all the things people are scared of when they try to kill themselves. On that happy note, I will tell you that I don't see anything inherently wrong in still living in Cleveland. I don't blame the mass majority of people I grew up with moving elsewhere, but I don't consider the ones who still live there failures in life either. Some people, for God knows why, actually truly like Cleveland. Clevelanders are the best people in the United States (Swiss are pretty nice and will give them competition on a world scale). With that being said, I have absolutely no idea why they would stay in Cleveland unless they're married and have children. Although my mom was born in New York, she grew up in Cleveland, married my father, moved back to New York, had two kids, moved to North Carolina, had two more, and then moved back to Cleveland to raise the four kids. Before they had kids, however, they were out of Cleveland. This is almost completely because my father went to Medical School in New York and then did his residency in North Carolina and my mom had kids during this time. Yet, something did convince my father to leave the city he went to undergraduate in (Cleveland) for his continued education. I went to New York for college and now I hope to never leave. The point is though: Living in Cleveland is not an indication that you have failed in life. And this is coming from someone who says what I said earlier about Cleveland. Kosta felt the need to bring up the fact that many of his attackers live in Cleveland. What does my brother believe about my parents who currently live in Cleveland? Are they now failures? His verbal assaults on everyone who attacked him who live in Cleveland makes it seem like living there is a bad thing. I'm completely baffled by this point. He also had the criticism that all these individuals work for their fathers and never independently made something of themselves; but, this is true about Kosta as well and the Cleveland point is just plain wrong.

The other conversation I had with my brother happened on New Years Day of 2005. I was a junior at NYU. I left my then best living friend's house in Norwalk, Ohio, drove the 45 minutes back to the western suburbs of Cleveland, picked up my suit, and then headed to the airport to pick up Kosta to accompany me on a two and a half hour drive to Pittsburgh for a wedding of a close family friend. The previous day, I had gotten into a huge fight with my friend in Norwalk and his father. Quickly, the father's issue with me was completely legitimate. I apologized both verbally and left him a written note the next day. My friend's issue was not justifiable. I knew driving away from that house that my six year friendship was over. I'm writing this on August 9, 2009. He and I have not hung out or been amicable to each other since that day, over four years ago. So I was right. Although I am not an emotional person, and I have lost contact with friends or had people tell me that they didn't want to be friends anymore before this incident, this was the first time it ever affected me. I was in complete shock. I lived at this kid's house for the better part of six years. To the point that the previous summers I had spent in Cleveland, I drove to New York frequently. The summer between my sophomore and junior years of college, I made the trip five times. Summer is only three months long, and on more than one occasion when I wore out my welcome at my friends' and family's houses in New York and was forced to drive back to Cleveland prematurely, I went to Christian (my friend's) house without stopping at mine. From my junior year of high school till that New Years 2005, (I graduated high school in '02) I spent almost all of my time when I was in Cleveland at his house. They even included me on family trips. Our whole friendship was completely thrown away in one night. I was absolutely stunned and in no position to argue. All defensive mechanisms I have relating to wanting and trying to be alone and pushing people away were gone. I was at one of my most vulnerable states of my life and I was trapped in a car for two and half hours with my brother.

This conversation would go on to be the most important conversation I had had with Kosta because he exploited my current state and talked at length about all the things he tried to tell me before, but I had never listened. He and I completely bonded. This, ultimately, is a good thing and made me kind of happy that things with Christian and his family went so badly. It's really more important to be close with siblings than with friends. I've been fine without Christian in my life for the past four years. Things would have been a lot harder without Kosta in my life.

I will never win any awards for my belief of the importance of family; but, in a perfect world, you should get along with your family, I just really don't.

I can't really dissect this conversation like I did the previous one. Kosta quoted two sayings that he said I should always live by, "God gave you two ears and one mouth for a reason" and "Knowledge is knowing the extent of your ignorance."

I have a belief that the hardest advice to take is your own and Kosta's failure to listen to those two quotations is the greatest example. Given that he talked at length about saying more using fewer words, not realizing the inherent contradiction, and the way he dismisses everything I say is proof enough that he never grasped the first quotation. The fact that he is incapable of seeing his failures in life shows that the second one never really hit home either. His point is true though; you should live by these quotations.

I will not go into any more specifics as his words were similar to the conversation at the diner. The difference was that I was almost five years younger, had less life experiences, and less confidence to speak against him. This shows how little he's progressed in that time and how much I've grown in the same amount of time. I will tell you what I took away from this conversation. I stopped viewing myself as the black sheep of the family and realized the phenomenon of unconditional love that my parents have for me, which is a concept that, to this day, I have not fully grasped. I realized my family is not my enemy and to not treat them as if they were. Now you may know that I do not speak to my sister and my younger brother, and, therefore you may say that I have not grasped this concept; yet, I don't consider them my enemies because they don't mean any harm. They just bring me down and detract from my doing what I want to do with my life. From that conversation with Kosta, I started to realize that my parents do know me and would go on to realize how similar I am to my father. The closest I got to this realization in the diner a week ago was when sitting across the table from Kosta; I noticed, for the first time, that he and I actually look alike. Kosta and I have both belittled some of his past girlfriends who have made this claim. I am a small framed, 6'0" not very hairy person with a shaved head,. Kosta has a darker complexion, and is 6'4" with a full head of hair, broad framed, and is extremely hairy. Maybe I have realized this because my head is shaved, and I can better see its shape and my facial features. Despite our other differences I just alluded to; Kosta's facial features are almost identical to mine. I saw my face in Kosta's, and that was very strange to me. I had grown up believing that I was the black sheep of the family, a sort of milkman's baby if you will. After that car ride to Pittsburgh with Kosta, I opened my eyes to the possibility that I was not just a member of my family by blood, evidence of which I have continually seen to this day.

It's not that I learned a lot from Kosta during that conversation; it's that I learned that I was wrong about a lot of things and had the foundation then to realize some long held beliefs of mine were wrong. With their destruction as a base, I have built upon them to get closer to reality. I expect this experience to continue throughout my life and I welcome it. Before that point, I would not have welcomed anything to attack my bubble I called my life. This newly held vision coupled with losing my fear of death has allowed me to experience and do many things with my life that has made me grow and mature as a person. It also allows me listen to Kosta when he speaks and then filter out the bullshit later. The fact that I have surpassed him in life experience makes our conversations less earth shattering than the car ride; but, I have now completely embraced the two quotations; I listen to people when they speak ("God gave you two ears and one mouth for a reason") and I continually inquire about everything I don't know and try to learn about these unknown things ("knowledge is knowing the extent of your ignorance.") It's not that that was the first time I had ever heard the quotations. I've known the Socrates quotation of "Knowledge is knowing the extent of your ignorance" for years, but, it was the first time I had ever strived to embrace and live them.

Although I spoke at length about the most recent conversation with Kosta, it is obvious to all which is the more important conversation. Also, my criticisms of Kosta can be applied to common fallacies with the world today. I have profound respect for Kosta's intelligence and life views; I just wish he could see himself from the outside and take his own advice. Because of the first belief, I am thrilled to talk with Kosta and will welcome all opportunities to have future conversations with him.

Now that I have attacked my brother so vehemently, I will mention some of his good traits. I am often guilty of only reporting the negatives about a situation. Because of this, I have learned to read over and focus on good things after giving my initial take. Kosta has helped me more than any other member in my immediate family. When I struggled to get a job after college, it was Kosta who convinced my parents not to ship me back to Cleveland. He even allowed me to live with him. Since I am the middle boy of a family of four, and the second child, my sister, is the only girl, I am the only one to suffer from being a middle child (the third). What I mean by this is my parents almost never listen to anything I have to say. When the issue would affect me negatively, I would call on Kosta to be a mediator. He would literally repeat my argument verbatim to my parents. After hearing my words from my brother's mouth, my parents would all of a sudden have a revelation that the point was sound. When I would complain about this, Kosta would just proclaim that it's just the way it is. Since he is the eldest, my parents listen to him and not to me; so, my arguments make sense from his mouth but fall on deaf ears from mine. To further explain my housing situation, my parents wanted to take away my Upper East Side apartment the second I graduated college. Kosta paid for it for another year and a half before he finally couldn't afford it himself. Therefore, he had me move in with him. When I decided to leave my family's business and go off on my own, Kosta was the only one who was extremely supportive of this decision. He has helped me in more ways throughout my life than merely giving me advice on a couple occasions. He has always been there when I needed him and has always been patient when explaining things to me if I didn't understand them the first time around. Some may view the negative things I have said about him as a slap in the face to him considering everything he's done for me. To me though, I have to be honest about him. The truth will take you to both negative and positive views, and not recognizing both would be dishonest. He will probably read these words and he, like many of you, will think it was very insulting, but I know the truth. Feel free to judge as you please.

By the way, if you were curious about the pattern mentioned previously, I will tell you the answer. I waited this long because I wanted to reward you for getting past the first chapter. To refresh your memory, the pattern is:

1
11
21
1211
111221

The next sequence is "312211." If you start at the first line and count the numbers writing down every number you say, you get each progressive line. You start with 1. If you count the numbers, you say "One one" in that, there is one number one. Since you said "one" twice, you write two ones, hence the second line. Now read the second line, "Two ones," in that, there are two number ones. Looking at the third line, you see that's what I wrote down. Each line follows the same pattern.

STEREOTYPES AND GENERALIZATIONS

As I write this, the title of this chapter is a hot topic now because President Barak Obama said an officer who was called to a house because they believed there was a break in was "acting stupidly" even after admitting that he didn't have all the facts. This immediately had a variety of people coming out against President Obama. The whole reason this got national news is that Bostonians made a big deal about this case because of "racial profiling." The point is, anyone who believes stereotypes and generalizations in and of themselves are bad is completely wrong. To put it more bluntly, you liberal scum bags who believe this are morons. Alright, now try to calm down and remember God gave you two ears and one mouth for a reason. You say you're open minded so try not to be hypocritical and be open minded to this chapter.

The human mind uses short cuts called "schemas" in order to process information. It does this as a survival mechanism so it doesn't have to start from scratch on every new experience. Without this, life experience would be worthless because you couldn't rely on past things you learn to apply to whatever new encounter you have. These "schemas" are generalizations and stereotypes. They're just different words for them. In psychology, when talking about neurons as they relate to schemas, they have something called the "Grandma" neuron. It asks the question,

"Do we have a neuron that says what our grandmother looks like?" Obviously, if the answer is yes, feel free to assume that you have one for everyone and anything you can identify. Since we have millions of neurons, this can be believable. They go on to explain how ridiculous this is when you filter in some other things. One being is that your grandmother looks different depending on what angle you're looking at her. Now, we do not have enough neurons to have one for every single possible angle you see your grandmother at so having a neuron for every conceivable position your grandmother can be in is not possible. Let alone having to duplicate this with everything and everyone you can identify. Your grandmother looks different from either side, the back, the front and every turned direction in between, which is infinite. A slight fraction of one degree shift makes her look different, yet you can recognize your grandmother consistently no matter what angle she's at. How do you suppose you do this? Your mind makes short cuts, it looks for some features unique to your grandmother and when it realizes these distinguishing features it tells you that it's your grandmother. In a sense, you have made a generalization and stereotype about what your grandmother looks like. Even when she cuts her hair, does it differently, or wears different clothes, you are not fooled most of, if not all, of the time, because you look for your stereotype for her. This is true for every person you have ever met.

Now, what's true for your grandmother is also true for groups of people. Let's start with the Greeks. It's easy to start with Greeks because in American society, you're allowed to make fun of Caucasians and Greeks are considered Caucasians. I choose Greek people because I am Greek so it's nice to start with things I know. My suitemate freshman year of college asked me, "If you know someone is Greek, what percentage of them do you think you already know?"

I thought about it and said, "25."

He immediately told me that was really high. I did not back down from the statement, nor do I now. I have almost never been surprised by a Greek person's actions. Once, I even predicted a Greek girl's actions whom I met once for 30 seconds and have consistently been right about her when my friend was wrong despite her longtime relationship with her. My biggest reason for being able to do this was knowing that she was 100% Greek in that both her parents were Greek.

Now, I can't really explain to you everything I know about Greek people because some things I just know but don't know how I know. I can't even fully explain how I predicted that girl's behavior so accurately and so consistently. If you want to know, read the book *Blink* by Malcolm Gladwell for the best description of this that I've read. Basically, because you've been around it for so long, you just know things. The one guide I will give you to Greek people is that Greeks are stubborn, loud (for White people), nationalistic, opinionated, think Greece is the greatest place in the world, wear black, father owned a diner, has a family member named a derivation of Kostandino (some American translations include Gus, Dean, Dino, Constantine) and do not see the hypocrisy in yelling at someone for never calling them when they never call that person either.

What I have just given you are stereotypes and generalizations. Like all stereotypes and generalizations there is not a single characteristic that every Greek person has. I also do not know of any Greek that possesses every single one of the stereotypes on the list. Here's what I will tell you though, I don't know many Greek people that don't have a majority of the items on the list. I remember being on the beach one time and having girls come up to us because we were talking about something very risqué. Somehow the fact that we were Greek came up (we probably told them without much prodding), they asked us if we knew this Greek person they knew. My cousin immediately said, "Yea, he's like olive skinned, family owns a diner and has a brother named Gus." The girls said, "Yea, Yea, that's him." Then debated whether or not he actually had a brother named Gus.

All of us knew that my cousin just rattled off some Greek stereotypes, but we fooled the girls. Maybe they were stupid, I just think we did give a pretty accurate description because stereotypes do describe about 25% of all Greek people and he was just able to verbalize a couple and it was enough for the girls to identify him. My point is that you need to embrace your stereotypes and generalizations about people but be responsible with them. Use it as a shortcut not a "Be all and end all." When I meet a Greek person, I mentally have my list and cross off the things that don't apply and add things that make them unique as humans. This is my shortcut for getting to know him or her and it works. If I just naturally assumed they were all true and didn't revise the list based on each person, then I wouldn't be responsible and wouldn't be right nearly as often as I am. For every race that I have encountered, I have a similar list either compiled by personal experience or from what was told to me by others. Obviously, you should take things heard from other people with a grain of salt, but inadvertently it makes it to my schemas. The point is, be responsible and use it as a guide to get to know someone. When you use stereotypes and generalizations responsibly, you can understand people better and quicker and save yourself a lot of time.

In the play *Avenue Q*, they have a song called, "Everyone's a Little Racist." Throughout the song, they come out against someone for being racist and then make a racist comment themselves. The chorus indicates that if everyone could admit that everyone's a little racist, the world would be a better place, and I agree.

For those of you who may have come back with, "Well, Greek stereotypes aren't that bad, what about Black and Hispanic stereotypes?"

Blacks and Hispanics having negative stereotypes are caused by the good Blacks and Hispanics who do nothing against the bad ones, which gives their race a bad name. When Chris Rock says, "There's a civil war against Black people, there's Black people and then there's Niggers." Based on his interpretation, I will make a highly racially charged argument. If Black people came out against n-words, the predominant stereotypes for Black people wouldn't be the same as they are for n-words. Liberals will tell you that there are crazy and bad apples in all groups. The difference is you have to research them for Whites, but Blacks you see on a regular basis. For those of you upset that I do not fully write out the n-word unless I'm quoting someone, please be patient as I address this in a later chapter. To further quote Chris Rock, "Blacks aren't crazy… if you hear a news story that a criminal tore out someone's eyes and used them as click clacks……White guy. If you hear that someone's in jail for stealing socks……. Black guy."

Chris Rock is using stereotypes but that doesn't make him a bad person. He's right. White crimes are extremely heinous, but how come people don't get worried when a White person is walking toward them on the street but they do when a Black person is? The easy argument would be a higher percentage of crime is caused by Blacks and Hispanics than by Whites despite making up a smaller percentage of the population. My answer to explaining both facts is the same: Whites are more deterred from crimes than Blacks. For those of you who think that capital punishment is not a deterrent, then why did they hang people in town squares for everyone to watch a couple hundred years ago? When you're in jail, especially in America where we have endless appeal processes, you always have a chance to get out. When you're dead, you're dead. White people and White judges will elect to kill White people for violent crimes. Death row is filled with White inmates and not many Blacks. A fact Chris Rock loves to point out. Civil Rights Activists will even call that racist because, "You only get the death penalty for harming White people but not Black victims."

This is completely negated when you look at the statistics. White violent criminals have White victims and Black violent criminals have Black victims. The difference is that Blacks are put in jail for a couple years and Whites are executed. I will admit that the White crime is usually more heinous but if a Black person were to commit the same crime, they wouldn't get the death penalty like a White person would because the judge would deem that decision racist. N-words are respected by their peers for dropping out of school, going to jail, and committing crimes. They also vilify Black people who rise above it. Blacks get no respect from n-words for graduating college or doing well in corporate America. This makes it less appealing for a Black person to strive for greatness. N-words keep Black people down. When Bill Cosby came out and told Blacks to stop blaming White people for their drop out rate and not advancing but instead to look internally, the Black community (I would call it the n-word community) came out against him. Although I do not like President Barak Obama, I applaud and commend him for giving a similar speech at the NAACP that Bill Cosby gave. It was very well received, and that is President Barak Obama's best accomplishment since he took office six months ago. White people do not let their crazy psychotic members run their race. Instead, they kill them, send them to the middle of nowhere in Colorado or Utah or put them in jail for life. Blacks let n-words take over theirs, and that is why general stereotypes for Whites are positive and general stereotypes for Blacks are negative.

Obviously, there's more than one race. Islamist terrorists are right now the highest scum of the Earth to me. They are a people that have no concept of mutual destruction, which kept the Cold War cold between Russia and America. These people do not care how much their country is bombed or ruined, so long as they can take a pound of flesh out of the great Satan that is America. Now, when I talk like this, people tell me that not all Muslims are terrorists. Of course they're not. I've met some Muslims who are extremely warm, compassionate and great to be around. They're also one of the most hospitable groups on Earth. The point is though, the good ones, who I will admit are the majority, do nothing to keep the fundamentalist crazy terrorists in check. Christians, on the other hand, are very good at keeping their fundamentalists at bay away from civilized society. Muslim terrorists blow up subways in Madrid, embassies, the Pentagon, the World Trade Center, public squares and basically anywhere there are a lot of people. The good people who practice Islam moderately, do nothing against the fundamentalists who kill people. Mormons, the Christian version of fundamentalists, kill babies, rape women if they refuse to marry and are downright horrible human beings. The reason why the *Southpark* creators Trey Parker and Matt Stone can get away with saying that Mormons are the only religion to make it to Heaven and nobody bats an eye is because Christians do a good job of making sure the general public doesn't know about the atrocities that Mormons commit. They put them in "nowhere" Colorado, Utah, and South Dakota so they only kill each other and don't get into mainstream America. If you read *Under the Banner of Heaven* by Jon Krakauer, you will get an in depth view of how horrible fundamentalist Christians aka Mormons are. My point is…you have to read the book and dig down. You don't have to look too hard to find the Islamist atrocities…. It's in your face. When Christians give swamp land or an undesirable place to live to Mormons and they, being as extremely hard working as they are, make it nice, the Christians/White people just go back, kick them out again and force them to start over. They treat their fundamentalists worse than any other group because they don't want them to give them a bad name. One exception to this is Catholic priests raping little boys. The Catholic Church has failed in disciplining them as they do serial killers and the Mormons. That is merely an exception to the rule that Christians and White people keep those that will give them a bad name out of mainstream society (or existence in the case of capital punishment) whereas Muslims do not. They would much quicker kill their promiscuous daughter to not bring shame on the family name than kill a terrorist for giving Muslims a bad name.

The opinion that I have gotten the most negative feedback on is the belief that Cleveland Arabs are horrible people. I lived in Cleveland for 15 years and I have never met one decent Arab in Cleveland. The fact that former President George Bush and the United States in general believe Saudi Arabia to be a friend scares me more than anything else. I met a number of Arabs when I lived in Cleveland and all of them were bad. People call me ignorant for saying such things that they're sure that they're not all bad. My point to them is: it is more ignorant to say that they're not all bad when you have never been to Cleveland nor met a Cleveland Arab. Only someone who has met a Cleveland Arab in their natural habitat of Cleveland can comment on them. To not do so, is just hearsay or ignorant. Since most of the people have never met anyone else who has commented on Cleveland Arabs, they're not even speaking from what they've heard or read, but a baseless assumption. Given that it can't be hearsay since they've never heard anyone say it, they're just ignorant. So, if you were offended by this paragraph and have never gone to Cleveland and met a Cleveland Arab, you need to shut up because you clearly have no basis in which to speak from….My 15 years living in Cleveland gives me the right to comment.

I left out Hispanics because everything I said about Blacks can be said about Hispanics with one major exception. The basic point that Hispanics do nothing to keep the people that give them a bad name in check is true. They don't condemn them or punish them severely the way White people do to their trash. The major difference is groups of Hispanics don't applaud and commend Hispanics who refuse to work or get out of jail. They simply ignore them. I would say ignoring is better than applauding and encouraging, but it's still not as good as condemning the way White people do. Hispanics are extremely hard working people and White people have been bitching about that since they came here. Hispanics are willing to work harder for cheaper means, and I commend those that do. If White people can't find blue collar jobs because they're not willing to pack eight of them in a house, or to work the long hours for little pay, then the Hispanic will and should win. This is why Hispanics are climbing faster than any other minority; deep down they're hard working people.

It isn't even a new strategy. When the Irish came to the U.S. because of the Potato famine, they were met with "No Irish Need Apply" signs. Did they bitch and moan? No, they did all the dirty and crap jobs that nobody else wanted and worked their way up through hard work. They even got a President in JFK.

The other thing I will say about Hispanics is that they are not as racist as Blacks are towards Whites. The argument that they were never slaves is noteworthy but slavery was two hundred years ago, it's time to move on with your bigotry.

Given that I have close Hispanic friends, I have often found myself the only White person among a bunch of Hispanics, but I have never been given a reason to be afraid. They would come up to me and say things like, "Oh you're White, you've never had platanos, here try this."

As the stereotype would suggest, since I am White, I cannot dance and I have no rhythm. The one thing that I find when someone forces me to go to a club or I'm forced to go out is if someone whom I've never met shows me how to dance, and is real patient with me, it's always a Dominican girl. Most of my close Hispanic friends are Dominican and I cannot explain why this is the case, and neither can they, but it is a fact. They will set a rhythm and then divert to me to lead (since they're still old fashioned and believe men should lead) but if I lose the rhythm, they'll find a way either by putting my hand on their waist or some other way for me to follow them just to get the rhythm back before going back to letting me lead. Hispanics love showing people their culture. Since Greeks can't wait to tell you about the history of their people, I can easily relate to this trait, which is why I'm so naturally gravitated toward Hispanics.

I've also been the only White in a Black neighborhood, and this sense of hospitality and opening of their culture is completely non-existent and I consider myself thankful and lucky to have not been harmed in those situations. There is not one time when I was the only White person among Hispanics where I felt this way. Since I know from personal experience that a large majority of Hispanics are good people (I can't say that about Blacks because the majority have been discriminatory toward me) I am more hopeful that they will do something to keep their bad seeds in place. Hispanics are good people and if the population trends continue and they do outnumber Whites in the coming decade, I will not be worried.

To close this chapter, I am extremely fascinated with other cultures. Since I've moved to New York, I have not made friends with anyone that is a mutt. The closest person to come to this, is a girl who's a mixture of a lot of nationalities but both her parents are Jewish. She isn't very religious but she identifies with it strongly. Although she'll argue that point, the fact that she would never marry a non-Jew says all I need to say about my saying she identifies with it strongly. I love to travel to other countries and speak with people of that culture so that I can make a list of stereotypes and generalization to continually revise and update it so that when I meet new people, regardless of their culture, I have a head start in getting to know them. Even though I'm introverted, meeting people is an inevitable fact of life, so give yourself the greatest edge you can. I have more trouble relating with someone who believes nationalism doesn't exist and is a variety of backgrounds and nationalities than any other group. Being Greek is such a large part of who I am that I am unable to understand what I call "Mutts." Luckily, I live in New York, where people embrace their cultures as they do in Europe. Also to my delight, America is the only country that thrives on being different, Greek-American, Italian-American, African-American etc. etc. In other countries their genealogy being from a different country doesn't stop them from considering themselves Canadian, English etc. etc. Their only concern generally is where they were born. If you can think of exceptions and argue against it, then you have missed the entire point of the chapter.

Homosexuals and Gay Rights

What bothers me the most about the debate for Gay Rights is that it's such a hot topic in today's society. I truly believe that Gay marriages will be legal across America in the near future. The reason being is that it's on the ballot every year, and even though it gets defeated every year, they just keep trying and one year they'll succeed then it won't be on the ballot anymore. What happened in the 2008 election is that Blacks came out to vote in record numbers to support Barak Obama. Most Black people are Christians and many of them are Baptists. Christianity is very clear on the issue of homosexuals and marriage. Marriage is a sacrament in which you are supposed to be fruitful and multiply. I don't care what position you're in, Gay sex will never produce a baby. They say, " Never say never." I'm saying….NEVER! In-Vitro fertilization is not having a baby through Gay sex. You merely have sex, and then go to a clinic to get a baby put in. How people argue that that's the same thing is beyond me. So, the Blacks generally voted against Proposition 8 to legalize Gay marriage. Gays then picketed and rioted out of White Catholic churches. The highest percentage group that voted against Proposition 8 were Blacks. Liberals could see this data, yet they chose White Catholics, I wonder why? Simple, society views Blacks as a more discriminated minority than Gays, so they would get no sympathy for picketing Baptist churches but they would for White Catholics.

Now, liberals will argue that they found the "gay gene". The gay gene is said to be found on the Xq28 stretch of the X chromosome. The problem is that not all people who consider themselves Gay have it and some people who say they're not Gay, have it. Now, if you believe it is a gay gene, then you have to say that those who don't have it that say they're Gay are lying, and those who have it but say they're straight are also lying. Unfortunately, no liberal stays consistent on this. The mere fact that liberals are going to genetics as an argument is completely hypocritical of everything else they believe. They believe gender is a social construct rather than genetic.

Well look, if you have a Y chromosome, you are a male. The hermaphrodites that have XXY, are males because they have a Y. I hate to include them in my race too, but hey, it's science. Transgender is not a sex. Your surgeries don't change your DNA and you've got to deal with it.

Liberals at NYU tore off the "Men" and "Women" signs in the bathrooms because it's discriminatory. It happened so often that NYU had to paint "Men" and "Women" on the doors. Shockingly, no vandalism of painting over the signs occurred as of 2006 when I graduated. These same liberals that claim gender is a social construct, claim that sexual preference is genetic. This is completely absurd. They also completely ignore the thousands of people who, after going to Christian counseling to stop their confusion of their sexuality, come out and are heterosexuals. Liberals say that they just claimed to be to get out and gave in to the torture but coincidentally, they never go back to being homosexual for the rest of their lives. I'm sure a liberal will say the Catholic Church just messed them up that much. If you believe this, I'm sorry, you're a moron. It's not genetic, it's people who experimented with their sexuality and realized homosexuality wasn't for them. Society allows women to do this all the time, but men are not. I particularly don't believe this is fair for men, because I believe all men should be treated equally but that's not the case.

I'm not saying that homosexuality is not genetic, I'm just saying there's a lot of evidence that argues against that. My personal experience would lead me to believe that the flip side of it being completely societal doesn't seem consistent either. So, I'm telling you now, I don't know nor do I care but since everyone argues so vehemently one way or the other, I'll say it doesn't matter. Nonetheless, they shouldn't get married and here's why.

Homosexuals are extremely promiscuous. The average homosexual couple lasts a year and half. Homosexuals have an average lifespan of 20 years less than heterosexuals. To give you a comparison, smoking only takes seven years off your life. So, a homosexual lifestyle is almost three times more hazardous to your health than smoking cigarettes. Reason being is that STD's are much more common in Gays than any other group by up to 1,000%. Just as how people should not be rewarded for smoking, people should not be rewarded for having a homosexual lifestyle for the same reasons.....It is hazardous to your health. The Gay and Lesbian Task Force, an organization devoted to making sure that Gays have the same tax breaks in business as heterosexuals, had to stop giving homosexual couples the same benefits as married couples because they broke up and married again too often. Slightly hypocritical and proves the point that due to their promiscuity and multiple couples, Gays should not be given the same benefits as married heterosexual couples.

Aside from the logical facts above, Gay marriage would also create a slippery slope. Gay friends of mine and their supporters attack me for saying this but that doesn't change its validity. Homosexuality and Beastiality were removed from the DSM-IV, the list of psychological disorders, at the same time. There is a legal precedence between linking homosexual behavior with other alternative sexual exploits. It is not fear-mongering when I say that if you allow Gay marriage, then the people who like having sex with goats and other animals will want the same benefits. The world has already seen PETA argue that animals are equal to humans and I do hear arguments that they should be married, (just not as widespread as the Gay Marriage debate). Of the two, I think Gay marriage has more of a shot, but it's in incremental victories. The other group that would start arguing is the North American Man Boy Love Association (NAMBLA). In case you can't tell by the name, these are people who argue not only for Gay marriage, but that you should be able to have intercourse and marry a minor when you're an adult. Basically, it justifies pedophilia. There are Lobbyists for this group as well and they're pushing hard to decriminalize pedophilia saying that minors are humans too and are capable of making consensual decisions about sex. When kids these days are losing their virginity at 14 and, as recently as my grandparents' generation, were getting married at 15, they may make ground on this. I pray they do not, but homosexuals are making progress with Gay marriage and liberals seem to complain until they get their way and they take any illogical position that may help. As I said earlier, I do not like children, however, I believe that pedophilia is absolutely repulsive and there is no punishment too severe for child rapists. I do not want them riding the heels of a Gay marriage victory. For those of you who think this is absurd, look at Roman Polanski who raped a 13-year-old girl, fled the country, and then got arrested in Switzerland over 30 years later. A lot of people felt sorry for him and even made the argument, "We don't know if it was rape because the 13-year-old may have consented." And the fact that she didn't want the case to continue fueled this debate. Sadly, most victims of pedophilia don't want to prosecute, therefore, by this definition, a lot of pedophiles are back on the street to rape more young children.

Now most readers will think I'm homophobic. I have had many encounters with homosexuals and I have trouble generalizing and making schemas for them. They're all completely different. It's fascinating. One Gay guy I met freshman year of college would have rants where he would say, "I fucking hate Flamers." Now I would point out to him that he's Gay so that comment was a little strange, and he responded, "I'm not a Flamer, I don't wear silk shirts and parade around flamboyantly!"

Based on him, one may think that Gays are like the Blacks, there are Gays and Flamers and Flamers give Gays a bad name. Upon further encounters, I have never met another Gay person like him, so this needs to be disqualified.

Another example is a girl I know who went to Smith and realized she was a lesbian. I would say that she became a lesbian because of her surroundings, but we're three years removed from college and she's still dating women so that's evidence against that. If you think I was being discriminatory for thinking that she would only be a lesbian till graduation, I'll let you know that this is so common at Smith that they have a name for them, "L.U.G." or "Lesbians Until Graduation." She came to New York one year for the Gay Pride Parade and she invited me to a party that her friend from Smith was throwing at her apartment. Now, I'm in a room filled with lesbian rugby players. Despite the fact that I do believe I can defend myself reasonably well, there was no way, even if I could hit women, that I would ever win this fight. These women were muscular and tough. I'm guessing tough because they play rugby and I don't care what gender you are, you have to be tough to play rugby. The topic came up about Gay marriage and my opinion. Before being invited, my friend asked me not to let my opinions be known because they would, "Kick my ass." I told her I wouldn't start the conversation nor bring it up but since I do not lie, if asked, I will answer honestly. She was very nervous when I came over for good reason...or so I thought.

I was asked point blank what I thought about Gays (they use the term to mean both women and men) and I told them, "I think it's absolutely disgusting and I'm grossed out when I see any Gays kiss."

"What about lesbians?"

"I think it's disgusting to see lesbians make out. If you guys started making out, I'd be grossed out."

"Really? That's awesome, I fucking hate when heterosexual guys get excited when we make out!!"

I was absolutely shocked at this answer. I just told them their lifestyle is disgusting to me and they took it as a good thing. We talked honestly about my views, they naturally didn't agree with me but they were very respectful and we had a civil conversation about it. In fact, my conversation with the rugby lesbians was infinitely more civil than the same conversations I've had with heterosexual liberals. By the same extension, my conversation with my male homosexual friend is always civil, he makes fun of me for the bestiality argument, (which he calls the goat argument) but we're still friends and very respectful toward each other. To be fair, I will describe someone who provides evidence for innate sexual preference.

Both he and his family are deeply religious. This was why he was afraid to come out of the closet at first. Although all outward appearances and mannerisms about him led people to assume he was Gay, the mere fact that he didn't admit it made me believe that he wasn't. I couldn't understand why someone at the college he attended, where a lot of the men are Gay, wouldn't admit it. I wouldn't go so far as to say that heterosexuality is frowned upon at his college, but there is absolutely no reason to be in the closet based on the atmosphere.

Everywhere you look, people are openly claiming and flaunting being homosexual. I failed to see the reality in that as a devout follower of religion where homosexuality is frowned upon, he fought because he felt he was betraying his culture. A couple years later, he came out of the closet. When he did, he was much more fun to be around. The whole point is that you shouldn't have to hide yourself from your friends. Keeping anything inside and suppressing who you are is not healthy. As of this writing, he and I are still friends.

When it comes to the innate argument about homosexuality, lesbianism holds the least amount of ground. Every lesbian I have asked, or even famous ones, all had a problem with their fathers. Even the most famous lesbian, Ellen Degeneres, was molested by her father. Case after case you see lesbians being molested by their fathers. You do not see the same thing in Gay males with their mothers or fathers for that matter. Maybe one day I'll find a female equivalent to my friend but I'm not getting my hopes up. If you're going to argue innate homosexuality, you stand a better bet with males, problem is, eventually, someone is going to figure out that it doesn't convert to females. There will be more on my cognitive dissonance on this in a minute.

Some readers may have decided to speculate my opinion of homosexuals. Well, I'll tell you. I completely understand lesbians and I'm jealous of Gay men. If you're a liberal reading this, pay attention because I'm going to argue how I am evidence of innate sexual preference. The Gay friend I mentioned earlier who said he hated Flamers made me jealous of Gays. Almost all the friends I've made in New York have been women. My female friends are very affectionate with me and, for the most part, are very comfortable around me. I have shared a bed with almost all of them, and many of them are not opposed to cuddling while sleeping together (not intercourse but sharing a bed). One has on several occasions gotten out of the shower and jumped into my arms. I'm saying all this because in every case, none of them were more affectionate with me than they were with the Gay guy freshman year. I'm using the comparison because a close Platonic friend vs. a Gay guy should be about even. It's not even close. Where they dance close with me, they literally straddled and wrapped their legs around Aaron (the Gay guy who made the anti-Flamer comment). Although I believe American dancing is a "vertical expression of a horizontal desire," there is no truer example than watching a girl dance with a Gay guy. Even my friend who is opposed to cuddling and outward displays of affection had her legs around Aaron while dancing.

As I watched girls jump all over him, I became insanely jealous. I considered saying I was Gay just so I would have the same effect. It's been my experience that a lot of girls want to try to convince Gay men not to be Gay any more through their hooking up with them. I heard many girls say this about Aaron. Aaron would always politely turn them down. The biggest problem was that Aaron looked heterosexual and, I'm told, is attractive. He broke a lot of hearts because he'd go to dinner with girls not realizing they believed it was a date and then when they came on to him he had to tell them he was Gay. I never tested the theory of claiming to be Gay so that girls would be more touchy with me partly because I do not lie and I am a horrible actor. I can't pretend to be something I'm not. Back in college though, I was jealous of Gay men because women absolutely loved them.

As for lesbians, it makes sense to me. Most people write this opinion off as me just being a heterosexual male but I do not believe this is subjective. Look at a woman then look at a man, and tell me which one do you think was created first and which is the improvement after the original model messed up? I believe in God, so I will substitute "God" for the Creator. Given that science has not explained completely how life came from nothing (when there's no life and then life appears this had to have happened) I will stick with God created man, even though the story of Genesis held to the same microscope as science doesn't add up either. Problem is, default always go to God. For thousands of years, God and gods have been used to explain the unexplained so I will continue the tradition. How I think it happened was God created man and said, "Hmmm not bad, but I can probably do better." He then created women and said, "Now that's more like it."

Women are just more attractive than men. Their bodies curve so perfectly, their skin is so smooth and soft and feels so nice to the touch. Their bodies just flow regardless of their size, it's absolutely incredible. Then you look at a guy, I mean the penis is absolutely disgusting. One of my female friends claim that the fact that they have to sit down to pee gives them an inherent disadvantage because they take longer in the bathroom giving them less time than men to accomplish things.

This is preposterous to me, and when I hear about Elektra complexes and "penis envy" I scoff. A penis is nothing to be envious of and neither is having testicles on the outside of our body. It's a natural target that is debilitating with even the slightest blow. Women do not understand what it feels like to be hit in the testicles. Anyway, this is a conversation about aesthetics. A women's groin region is much more appealing because the subtraction of the penis, is an addition to her beauty. My theology teacher in high school once said, "If you ever feel arrogant, look down."

I honestly think a penis is the most disgusting looking thing on either human body. Women have breasts, and they're not like man boobs, but they're proportioned on each side of their body, stick out beautifully and just seem natural. The invention of halter tops and low cut shirts is proof that breasts are nice to look at. There's no revealing clothing to accentuate male genitalia for good reason. Women get tattoos on their bikini line to draw attention down there, you don't see this in men. Even when you look at the men who are commonly viewed as attractive like George Clooney, Tom Brady and Matthew McConaughey they have feminine features. They're smooth skinned and clean shaven. They have feminine features and females are finding that attractive. Women do not believe men when they say that we don't find men attractive but we honestly don't. If we do, we're looking for feminine features. Every guy I have conceded is attractive has smooth skin and isn't hairy. The interesting this is women will agree that these guys are attractive. I do have one Polish friend whose opinion in men's attractiveness is far different from mine. She believes Gerard Butler is hot. I've heard women remark that Ben Roethlisberger of the Pittsburgh Steelers is hot. I'm happy when I hear that because I believe they're being consistent when they say they're heterosexual (actually my friend says she's asexual but I believe her opinion on guy's attractiveness is evidence to the contrary).

I've heard men and some women argue that men are more attractive in older age. Yes, women lose their beauty and the gap in attractiveness between an older woman and when she was young is a lot more drastic than the same comparison with men, but women never drop down to their male counterparts. Men stay rather consistent but in the end, they're still below women in attractiveness at any age.

Aside from attractiveness, I don't understand what a girl gets out of being with a guy. The example I give is that there is no more manly feeling than hugging a girl and having her head against your chest and feeling her body completely relax. Men talk about picking up heavy things or opening cans as feeling manly, and it is, but nothing compares to that. Now when I hug my brother, it sucks because now my head is even to where most girl's heads are on me and it's very uncomfortable. I absolutely despise it. When I make this remark to my female friends they respond, "Oh, my God, do you know how good it feels to just feel so secure in a man's arms, I love it!" They add ecstatic noises to emphasize their point.

My response is always, "No, I have absolutely no idea what you're talking about."

So when a girl says she's a lesbian, I understand. I will never fully understand women, both lesbians and heterosexuals alike, but of the two, lesbians make more sense to me. How could you ever be attracted to a man? Given this opinion, it's easy to extrapolate what I think of homosexual males… Completely baffled.

New York Men

Since I've moved to New York I have noticed that, unlike my time in Cleveland, almost all of my friends are girls. I attributed this to having gone to an all boys Jesuit Catholic high school in Cleveland. When exposed to both males and females, as I was at NYU, girls would win out. The problem is this doesn't explain the male friends I made during my 11 years I lived in Cleveland and did attend co-ed schools. The new conclusion I have come to is that a vast majority of the men who grew up in New York, and were born after 1978, have turned into effeminate metrosexual cowards.

That isn't exactly how I describe them verbally. I replace the word "coward" with a word that when followed by "willow" describes a certain plant. I feel that that word should not be written here despite my hatred for euphemisms. Now, this may be a shocking conclusion to many of you, especially the ones who do not live in New York, but my experience has told me that this is overwhelmingly true. Non-New Yorkers especially may think this because when they watch TV and hear stereotypes, New Yorkers are always portrayed as aggressive, violent, rude and always close to snapping and fighting. New York men feel they need to portray this stereotype when they leave New York on vacation, but once they're back here, they revert back to being a metrosexual coward. How people act in their natural habitat, i.e. where they call home, is more evidence to how they really are. If you don't agree, than you can continue believing that New York men are as advertised. But, in New York, it is not uncommon to find guys who get manicures and pedicures, wax their backs, enjoy shopping and spend hours upon hours in the bathroom grooming themselves while they get ready to go out. This simply does not happen in any other culture I've witnessed.

Now, just because there's one feminine thing about someone doesn't earn them the title of "Metrosexual Coward." For those of you that have never heard the term "metrosexual" before, it basically means a male who claims to be sexually attracted to females but acts like a homosexual. I believe that almost all guys and girls have some characteristics that are more typical of the opposite sex. In order to earn the title of "Metrosexual Coward," you have to possess more feminine traits than male traits. Here are some examples......

Like most college students, I lived in a dorm when I first got to college. Then, when I graduated and started making my own money, I couldn't afford to live alone in New York City so I got a roommate. I've moved eight times and have had seven places I've called my place of residence (I moved to the same place on two separate occasions). Every time that I have lived with a guy who grew up in New York, I've had the following things said to me, "Why didn't you call me to tell me you weren't coming home for dinner? Why didn't you tell me you weren't coming home tonight? And, You never show any emotion toward me." You can judge whether that's something a heterosexual guy would say to his male roommate. I am not romantically involved with any of them, nor did any of them want to be, but this is the shit I'd have to listen to. My reaction is to just tell them, "If I'm not here and you want to eat, eat without me. Don't worry if I don't come home, and you're my roommate not my friend." Normally followed by, "You're not my wife or mother, stop acting like a girl."

When my roommate from Cleveland moved in with me, he never told me what time he was going to come home, or if he'd be home for dinner or anything of that nature. I never called him asking these things either. If I was home and he was too, great, if not, I'd do my own thing. He did the same. That is how male roommates should act. I'm not talking about someone I hardly knew; this is my closest friend alive right now. Despite how well we get along and how good of friends we are, we feel absolutely no need to make these phone calls.

During my time here in New York, I've had a few male friends. Keyword in the previous statement is "had." I will admit I treat women and men a little differently. I try not to, but certain things are inevitable. I have infinite patience if a woman acts like a woman. I have absolutely no patience when a man acts like a woman. The women in New York, by contrast, are normally really strong and less sensitive than the females in Cleveland. In a sense, they're more masculine than the women in Cleveland but most of them still act like women in the end. The thing is I don't mind if a woman has predominantly masculine personality traits, I do mind if a man has predominant feminine personality traits. This is always what caused my friendship with the men to go south and end.

Despite almost all my friends in New York being women, I have seen my former male New York friends cry a lot more than my female friends. This just shouldn't happen. Midwest men do cry, but that's extremely rare. Women normally cry a lot more than men. I've heard women say, "I had a good cry."

Thankfully, I've never heard a guy say that, not even a New York one. But, I'm shocked at how frequently my former male New York friends would cry. One also would buy me multiple drinks so that I was on the verge of passing out so that he could put me in his car and take me home to Long Island with him because he didn't want to drive alone. Besides the obvious that you shouldn't drink and drive, this enraged me. You could argue that I shouldn't have drunk so much but I do not turn down drinks others buy for me. A fact he knew and exploited. Because of this, I had to stop being friends with him. For those of you who read that story and commented how Gay it sounded or have the assumption that he was trying to date rape me, you now see my point. Now, I wasn't raped any time with him, but it proves my point because most people get this image.

One of my male friends just visited me from Cleveland. He didn't believe me when I told him about New York men. Then he looked around the bar we were at and started seeing pop collars, a little too well-groomed men and men dancing with each other. We went bar hopping and found more of the same. This was in Brooklyn, which is supposed to be the toughest of all the New York boroughs. This was one of the reasons I decided to leave Queens and move to Brooklyn. Unfortunately, Brooklyn men act just like Queens and Manhattan men. I guess I can only report on those three boroughs because those are the boroughs I've lived in. I don't know many people who live in the Bronx or Staten Island. So, they get a pass for now. The men I've witnessed come from Brooklyn, Queens, Manhattan and Long Island. My friend was in culture shock because in the Midwest, men do not dance with each other, spend hours getting ready and such. When I brought this up at work, two women immediately disagreed with me. We argued about how men are supposed to act and one commented, "We're two women talking, we know what we're talking about."

Immediately I saw the root of the problem. That comment makes absolutely no sense anywhere except New York. A man should not take advice on how to act like a man from a woman. What will happen is they will become metrosexual, which seems to be the result. Somewhere, New York men born after 1978, got the idea that they should look to a woman on how to act like a man. That may show their lack of another stereotypically male characteristic...... Logic.

Before moving to New York I always believed that I needed to watch what I say because I may get in a bar fight. I kept hearing about these bar fights before moving here. I do tend to get loud and obnoxious when drunk, so I thought that this would be a problem. I was completely wrong. Despite my being loud, drunk and obnoxious at bars all over New York, nobody ever says anything to me. I haven't even been close to getting in a fight. Immediately the words from *Fight Club* came to me where they say, "Picking a fight with someone is not as easy as you would think. Most people will do anything to avoid a fight."

There is no city where this is truer than New York. If you're wondering what happens when I drink back in Cleveland, well, people are not as submissive. I still have never been in a bar fight but I have had people confront me with outward signs of aggression and tell me to, "Shut the fuck up!" I have not been to many bars in Cleveland, not nearly the amount as New York given that I've been living in New York for college years and after, which is before and after the legal age of drinking. Yet, nobody has ever tried to put me in my place or shown any forms of outward aggression in New York, and most of the times

I'm out in Cleveland, someone has. This is directly linked to the fact that Cleveland has real men in it and New York doesn't.

Aside from the fact that men take advice from women on how to act like men, you can see another possible route when you hear the pre-1978 people talk about their children's activities. They will complain about chatter in little league and trash talking in other sports. Where I come from, if the other team is screaming "Hey batter batter" or other forms of chatter, you crush the next pitch and get a base hit or more and suddenly the chatter stops. It's magical that way.

If in football someone gets in your face because they scored a touchdown, they don't talk so much when you march down the field and score on them. Also, they don't say much when you bat the ball down before they have a chance to catch it.

When someone nails a shot over you in basketball, quickest way to shut them up is to go back down court and score on them. Or, next time you're on defense, you block their shot. This is how we deal with trash talkers and chatter where I come from. In New York, the parents just whine and complain to the umpire and have gotten it banned in little league. Teach your kids how to deal with criticism and setbacks, not ban youths' freedom of speech. If you shelter them from all forms of controversy, they will grow up to be metrosexual cowards.

Some psychologist may say that I have some repressed feminine issues or some mumbo jumbo like that. This is why I'm going to include my one feminine characteristic. As I said earlier most men have at least one feminine characteristic, mine is that I love "chick flicks" a.k.a. romantic comedies. All you have to do is ignore the end when the couple gets together and focus on the previous hour and twenty five or so minutes and how funny it was. My friend who visited me irons his T-shirts, that's his one female characteristic. This is to emphasize my point before, just because a guy has a couple feminine characteristics, doesn't mean they're metrosexual, it has to be a majority. If you're still unclear, take a trip to New York, stay away from Times Square, Herald Square and other tourist zones and observe New York men in their natural habitat.

The last point about this topic I will make describes how frustrated I am by this….. I was at my friend's wedding in Cleveland. I had met his best man for the first time at the bachelor party a month before and, while talking to him, we were having a conversation on a topic that is very common when men talk to each other without the company of a woman: Masturbation. It was on a broader topic that I was single and loving it because I don't have to deal with the drama of a girlfriend. He then told me, "Well if you didn't have such smooth feminine hands, you wouldn't enjoy masturbating as much and you would realize the need for a wife."

Most people would find that comment offensive. To me, I just smiled and felt happy to be in a place where I'm considered effeminate for something. The fact that my reaction to an insult was relief, shows how frustrated I am with New York men. Hopefully, the Midwest doesn't become as metrosexual as New York. That way, on the seldom occasions I return to the place I grew up, I can get my relief to actually talk to men my age who act like men.

President Obama and the Dramatic Shift of America in 2009

I have thoroughly enjoyed President Obama's fall from grace. When he took office in January of 2009, he was the first president to ever be on Forbes top 50 celebrity list. His approval rating was at around 70%. I have never seen New Yorkers so happy as on the day after the election. It was a time of hope and change as I saw T-shirts and hats promoting Obama. I was astounded.

I do not like Obama. I voted for McCain because I do not like socialism, and Obama ran on a socialist ticket disguised as "Democrat." There really is no difference between the two. Given this atmosphere, I feared for the country because Obama, with Democrats controlling the house and Senate and the animosity toward Bush, was in a position where he could do no wrong. Add to this the fact that he was Black, and any time you criticize a powerful Black-man, immediately you're considered a racist. Obama would have a ball in the White House. Even more evidence of this is Obama's charismatic speaking ability. I haven't seen this since Bill Clinton. Even before the election was nearing, reporters were interviewing the Saturday Night Live cast and other comedians about how if Obama wins it make their job harder because of how cool he is. Even Chris Rock, who I have in my 3-way tie for most brilliant person I've heard speak, said it was difficult because, "He's just so cool."

I wish he was cool and had good ideas. So I feared for the country. As of this writing, (it is August 2009,) I seemed to be dead wrong.

I have been listening to town hall meetings where the mob and general public are berating Democrats all across the country as they completely opposed "Obama-care." Obama has already raised the national debt a trillion dollars. To those of you who just blamed Bush, I will repeat it in different words: The national debt is over a trillion dollars higher now than when Bush left office. That's when people first started turning against Obama. That and Obama is on TV talking all the time. In fact, some networks have refused to show him because every time they interrupt their broadcast to air a presidential speech, they have to reimburse their sponsors. Normally this is outweighed by how many people are tuned in to watch, but when it happens all the time, people don't watch as much and it's less cost-effective to have the president's speech. Add to this that Cap and Trade failed to go through….. Obama was off to a bad start. Now with his socialized health care plan, his popularity is down to 42%. I would never have guessed that in January and I have absolutely no explanation for it. Everything I mentioned before, I didn't think would be enough to do it and here's why.

I thought the national debt would be attributed to former president Bush for at least two years. I also thought since Obama is a great speaker, it wouldn't matter how often he spoke, people would listen. Since he campaigned about health care that resembled socialism, trying to push it through seemed only logical. Add to this the people who voted for Obama (presumably because of his campaign) would support him when he implemented the things he said he was going to. But they haven't. For those of you who believe that the town halls are organized by far right wingers, you may have a tiny point, but the fact that the crowd agrees, cheers them on, and speaks out should make you realize that they are conveying the mood of America. The right and the left have people who organize protests, the left is more violent because they throw pies and things, whereas right wingers stick to facts and logic. But, this is to be expected because logic is almost always on the right-winger side. I've asked liberals why people are turning against Obama because I just don't understand and they say, "Well everyone thought he was the Messiah, and now they're realizing he's not."

I'm astounded by this. I knew liberals weren't the smartest people on Earth but did you really believe that a presidential candidate would be the Messiah? Really? Come on. I don't even say that about former president Reagan, and he's my all time favorite president. Let me enlighten you about politicians, they will never ever be the Messiah. I wouldn't even call former mayor Giuliani, who magically cleaned up New York and put it on track to become the safest big city in the world, the Messiah. He's probably the closest any politician will get, but he's had some issues in his personal marriage and other things that make him fall short of the Messiah. Nevertheless, I can go on the subway at any time of night, and walk around the city I call home feeling safe. I don't care what Rudy Giuliani does, I will always love him for that. Especially when you see the Chris Farley skit making fun of him when he took over as mayor by insinuating he couldn't control his nephew, let alone crime in New York. Well SNL, you were wrong…funny skit though.

The only thing I can think of to explain the sudden drop in popularity is that people thought he was lying in his campaign. I will call President Obama a lot of things ranging from communist to terrorist sympathizer but he is not a liar. Now, one of his economic advisors has said that he will have to raise taxes on people who make less than $ 250,000.00 a year, which he repeatedly said he would not do during his campaign. As of this writing, however, he has not done that so until he lies, I'm not calling him a liar. He's doing everything he said he was going to do. He raised taxes on the wealthiest individuals, he lowered them on middle income to low income people and he wrote a 1,000+ page bill to the house and a 600 + page bill to the Senate to socialize health care. He didn't say how long it would take in the campaign, but he said he'd do away with insurance companies. He said he'd make it like Europe and Canada. He said all the roundabout circuitous ways to say that it's a socialized healthcare system. The fact that 70% of people who approved of him in January despite him saying all this, made me believe that when he actually tried to do it, the same 70% wouldn't be bothered and the 30% who were bothered, like me, would still be fearful. My question to the 70% is, "Did you think he was lying before?"

It isn't just with healthcare that Obama got attacked for something he said during his campaign. Cap and Trade failed to be passed because countries around the world refused to limit their emissions by shooting themselves in the foot. American corporations didn't really want to either and people realized how it was a "con." Government run corporations and government-friendly corporations would profit with every tax on emissions. When looking at the evidence, it may be surprising to you that I'm shocked it didn't go through but it goes along with my point. Obama said he was going to do this. Why weren't the 70% of people who approved of him after he became president mad at him before when he said he was going to do this? What took so long? Did you think he was lying? Please, for the betterment of the country, don't just naturally assume someone is lying. I know you can argue that all politicians lie, but rather than just assume they're lying, assume they will actually try to do what they say they're going to do and judge them on that. We could have avoided this whole thing if people just believed Obama would try to do exactly what he said he'd do about Cap and Trade and healthcare. My fellow Americans, please make the leap of faith that the presidential candidate is not lying and if he turns out to be lying, then crucify him for it.

Now, all the media outlets except Fox News have acted predictably. This helps my sanity because they are calling anyone who opposes President Obama racist, right wing nut, crazy, and stupid, which is the only point a liberal ever has when arguing with a conservative. At least that's predictable but every time they do that, their ratings plummet even more and Fox News raises even more. The pulse of America is leaning toward the middle or right and away from the left wingers. Now it's my turn to be happy. I even had the president of the Black Economic Board yell at a Democratic senator for being racist because she brought a quote from the NAACP in a debate about Cap and Trade. I knew the Democrats were the real racists, but to actually have a Black man say it was awesome. When Bill O'Reilly had him on and played devil's advocate, the man said in response to O'Reilly saying that she would say she loves Black people: "She loves Black people in their place. She loves poor Black people." Replace "she" with "liberals" and you have one of truest statements ever made.

In case you forgot, President Obama was real close to Bill Ayers, a domestic terrorist who bombs places in America, and Jeremiah Wright, who is a racist preacher. President Obama's wife said, "This is the first time I like America." Socrates said, "Show me your friends and I'll tell you what type of person you are." Well the world hasn't changed much in 5,000 years. Look at Obama's friends and the woman he chose to marry and ask yourself what type of person he is. Now that the whole "Messiah" image is gone, please judge him as a man so you don't make the same mistake in 2012.

It is easy to explain why the nation is shifting right. Once people see how liberals run the country, they demand a real conservative and, the party that's not in power organizes protests. When Bush was president, liberals organized protests monthly at NYU... and the rest of the country wasn't too far off. They would even create protests by telling the media that hundreds of people would file to protest at a place. Then, when journalists showed up and found six people with signs, they would wait a while to see if the protest was just late or they were misinformed. When journalists' are present, people start talking about how there's a bunch of TV cameras at a location and begin telling their friends. People, being as curious as they are, come to see why there are cameras, then when they see the cameras go up, the organizer invites them to the protest, they join so they can be on TV and voila the media has created a protest. The left is very good at this. The Leadership Institute tries to do the same with conservatives but they actually organize like-minded people first, then convince them to go out and protest and it's well on its way before the media shows up. I used to work for the Leadership Institute and they never did throw anything at speakers. They've organized to get up and leave to make it seem like people aren't interested, but liberals literally throw pies at Ann Coulter. The left also undermines speakers in the same way. You see more right wingers speaking out now because they're not in power anymore. The previous eight years you saw more left wingers doing it because the president was Republican. I think it's going to keep going like this beyond my lifetime.

Sarah Palin

I love Sarah Palin. The reason I love Sarah Palin is because she pisses off so many people. I've always believed that if someone can engender so much emotion either way, they're honest people. If I meet someone that everyone likes and has no enemies, I automatically think that person is fake. Elie Wiesel said, "The opposite of love is not hate........ it's indifference."

Ask anyone about Sarah Palin, you will not get indifference. I will go through some of her criticisms and talk of their legitimacy or lack thereof.

People say she's a bad mother. This is my favorite one because people don't seem to think of the implications of this statement. They say, "When you have five kids, you should not run for office, that's being a bad mother."

Well some of her kids are grown up and don't need her to raise them anymore and can help out with the younger ones. I don't know why her husband can't help with raising the kids, isn't it a progressive thing to say that woman can work and the men can help take care of the kids? Progressive is normally liberal, so I don't understand why they make an exception for Sarah Palin. Actually I do, liberals will always contradict themselves when a conservative exemplifies everything they've been fighting for. Liberals fight for women's advancement and women's rights so long as the woman is liberal or a democrat. Liberals were angry that just when Nancy Pelosi, a Democratic woman, reached the highest office any woman had held, the Republicans were going to one up them by having a female vice-president. They just couldn't stand for that, so they fought hard. Unfortunately, John McCain drank the Kool-Aid. He told Sarah Palin not to take the offensive or criticize Barak Obama so much. You know, listen to the liberals and don't be so mean. Let Obama say what he wants, we'll take the high road. Look where the high road got you McCain.

What happened after the campaign? Sarah Palin resigned as governor of Alaska shortly after. That was the only thing I've ever held against her. But I did not have to wait long before Sarah Palin came roaring back with one e-mail. She single handedly took a major part of Obama's health care bill off the table with two words: "Death panels." As soon as she said that, the public rallied against it, and the Democrats caved. How the hell did a private citizen do that? She had resigned and her political career was ending. (Some say she was going to save it for the president but normally politicians hold on to it until they win, not four years before running). Yet, single-handedly, she affected Obama's health care bill, an essential part of his campaign. I wonder what would have happened if McCain hadn't reined her in and let her go off. Maybe we'll find out in 2012.

If you're a liberal reading this I'm shocked because you guys don't like being attacked nor do you like facts or rationality, something this book is riddled with. But maybe you yelled at the book, "What about Katie Couric?"

One, stop yelling at the book, I can't hear you. Two, I'll address that. Sarah Palin couldn't name a Supreme Court case she disagreed with instead of Roe v. Wade. Well, I've never seen another politician be asked such a question, and I doubt most politicians would fare too well in that category unless they had a law degree. She also said she reads all the newspapers. Why did Palin pander to what the media wanted? Who the hell knows, maybe McCain told her. What she should have said is, "I don't read liberal propaganda and lies. Therefore, I do not read mainstream newspapers such as the New York Times or Washington Post. I get my news from credible news sources such as Fox and talk radio." Would she be admitting a right-wing agenda? Yes, but who cares.

Obama admitted being associated with a known terrorist in Bill Ayers and nobody cared. I don't think Sarah Palin reads the papers, and I like that about her. It shows she hasn't been corrupted by the liberal media.

Now for the double standard, the 2008 election pitted Barak Obama/Joe Biden vs. John McCain/Sarah Palin. The most vague way to describe this is: Democrat candidate inexperience/experience vs. Republican candidate experience/inexperience. For those who couldn't follow. … Barak Obama, the Democratic presidential nominee, was inexperienced in politics and Joe Biden, the democratic vice-presidential candidate, was very experienced to balance him out. The Republicans flipped it by having the experienced candidate as president and the inexperienced as vice-president. Logically, this makes sense but that's redundant because logic is almost always on the right side of the line. Let's remember, Joe Biden is supposed to be the guy who is experienced and knows how the world works. He says, "When the stock market crashed in 1929, FDR got on TV the next day and took control saying this is what we're going to do."

I say this to Obama/Biden supporters and they see nothing wrong with it because they absolutely refuse to question what a Democrat says. Here's the problem morons ….. In 1929, when the stock market crashed, Herbert Hoover was president, and there was no TV. I'm sure you may have been able to figure that out if Palin said it rather than Biden, but Palin didn't. John McCain didn't say anything stupid during the entire campaign…good for him. If you don't think Barak Obama did, well he did say, "I never heard Jeremiah Wright say anything controversial."

Well….he was a member of his church for 20 years, and I highly doubt that Jeremiah Wright only had the one outburst that was aired all over the place. During his rant, he called America the U S of KKK. Perhaps Obama never listened when he was in church, something that many people would relate to but Wright talks pretty loud. I doubt you could tune him out. Hopefully in 2012 Sarah Palin will be president. And just to be clear… no I do not believe she is the Messiah and will not be disappointed if she becomes president and turns out not to be the Messiah. I wouldn't want to make the same mistake as the Obama supporters would I?

MARRIAGE, HAVING CHILDREN, & SEX

Before I begin this, I need to give a little bit of background about myself. I do not want to get married and I consider myself asexual. Now, many people have a lot of definitions of "asexual". My definition is "someone who has lost the desire for sexual intercourse." I know psychologists are licking their chops over this. They'll come up with all sorts of shit, probably making absolutely ridiculous accusations about my parents. One, my parents never sexually abused me. The problem that the psychologists now have is that they will accuse me of repression, not understanding what's okay parental love or some bullshit like that. Even though I was a psychology major, I do not understand things that are completely illogical, retarded and just plain bullshit, which is what the field of psychology is. Now that I have attacked them, I will throw them a bone that they can run with. During the first semester of my sophomore year or college, I went to the Conservative Political Action Committee (CPAC) in Washington D.C., where I was molested by a secret service agent. To keep the story brief, my friend, whom I was rooming with, had met him while she worked at the Republican National Convention in New York, met up with him for drinks in D.C. and I joined them later. He went back to our hotel room. I thought he was trying to get with my friend, so I went to sleep knowing that I would be able to sleep through anything they would do. I woke up with his hand on my penis. I threw his hand off, he kept putting it back. I got up, went to my friend's bed and held her close to me and then he left the hotel room. His first name was Tom. I do not know his last name. This is not the moment I became asexual, that moment would happen two years later. I included this story because if someone were ever to uncover it, they could point to me, "Repressing it!" Here …. I've printed it in a public forum. It would be semi-easy to uncover since I've told many people about it. The question I get from guys the most is, "I would have fucking killed that dude, why didn't you?"

I consider myself someone who is not opposed to violence. I do believe that given he was a secret service agent he could probably kick my ass, but I do not believe that's the reason I didn't attack. To be honest, I don't know. Part of me believes I was just too tired and too shocked to fully react to what was going on. To the people who call me a coward for this, I'll just say, you have no idea how you would react until you wake up with a guy's hand on your dick. I can say this because if I heard someone tell me the story, I would have told you I would kick my leg back into his nuts and take the chance of getting my ass kicked… but I didn't. I also hope you're never in that situation.

Two years later I lost my virginity. It was a sorority girl who I had met for the first time at a club. I knew her sorority sister from three years ago but I hadn't talked to her in three years and we were never friends. Unlike most people, the sex lasted a long time, and it was extremely boring. Most people tell me that everyone's first time sucks but my question to them is why would you keep doing something you don't enjoy? With the exception of alcohol, I have never continued doing something that I did not enjoy the first time trying it. In the four years since I have renounced sex, my life has been a lot less dramatic and frustrating. Despite everyone I talk to being vehemently against my position, it is not something I regret.

To those of you who say that I'm not asexual because I admit that I was once heterosexual and turned asexual and that isn't how it works. I'll say, see the chapter about Gays and lesbians, it is a choice, not genetic. Ironically, the only person to ever believe me about my asexuality and not give me shit is my Gay friend. I commend him for that and am eternally grateful.

Now that the whole debate of whether or not I'm saving sex for marriage is out of the question, I will talk about marriage. I have often wondered why people get married. My parents have the best marriage that I have ever witnessed. Anyone who believes love fades has never met my parents. I've heard my mom come home as giddy as a 16-year-old whose crush just talked to her. On one occasion at the dinner table my mom said with a huge smile, "Guess what happened to me today? I got hit on."

I looked over at my dad and saw that he was not upset or angry but just kind of like, "Why is she telling this story?"

And sure enough, the story was my dad pulling his car next to her, complimenting her and trying to get her to take her sunglasses off. My mom refused and played hard to get. This is approximately 20 years into their marriage. Most people would find this nice, I think it's ridiculous. Love is supposed to fade, but my parents are on year 31 and I have seen no fading at all. They are not public about it as they will tell me, and I agree. Public Displays of Affection (PDA) is usually a sign of problems behind closed doors. One reason I don't like talking about how disgusted I am that my parents have such a good relationship is because my friends whose parents are divorced look at me like they want to kill me. I will say this, I'd much rather have my parents get along as well as they do than for them to be staying together just for us kids or being divorced. I talk about my parents because I don't want you to think that I see their relationship and am scared by it. Psychologists will come up with a couple of things for this A) I'm lying, repressing and that bullshit or B) I have an inferiority complex that I could never have a marriage as good as my parents. Both are false, and later I will tell you how to have a marriage like my parents. After all, if you insult something you should know about it. I will first tell you why I don't want to get married.

Marriage is never beneficial to the husband. Look at every single comedian or any person to ever speak on marriage. I'll quote Chris Rock since he said it most concisely and accurately, "Men don't decide to get married, we surrender."

Most married men will tell you that they said they'd never get married, then they met a girl who got them to surrender to marriage. Now, here I am saying I will never get married. Will a girl make me submit? I hope not, but it's possible. Luckily the girl that I believe had the best shot is getting married a little less than two months after I'm writing this chapter. American society is set up so that women get everything in a divorce. Think about what is automatic to the woman so long as she uses sentences that start with, "I'm accustomed to" (stolen from Chris Rock). They get the house, the car, the kids and half of everything you make whether or not she has a job or not. After all, behind every successful man is a strong woman. I hate that quote, because all you really do is point out that these successful men are married. Most people are married. Women are attracted to wealth because it gives them security, so where the fuck does the surprise come in that successful people are married? The women are never really that strong, I wouldn't call Ivana Trump strong. People just assume the woman is strong because the male is successful and they take the quote as a given. This is completely unfair to the man. Why does she get the house? Why do I have to move out?

Let's move on to the kids. I understand that babies have an innate attraction to the mother and not the father and vice versa. I also understand that women are better nurturers than men even if the feminists argue against this. However, I doubt these scientific studies when you see how fathers react when you ask them about their kids. Why does a father's love just get thrown out the window in exchange for a mother's love? That doesn't seem fair to the husband at all. The common rebuttal to this is to sign a prenuptial agreement. Let me translate a prenuptial agreement for you because I hate euphemisms and I call things what they are. A prenuptial agreement uses fancy language to say, "Hey baby, I love you, I want to spend the rest of my life with you, but I don't trust you at all so just in case you've conned me and try to screw me, sign this piece of paper so it's harder for you to do it."

If you sign a prenuptial agreement you are admitting you don't trust your spouse, and that is getting the marriage off to a bad start. If you don't believe me just look at the statistics that as prenuptial agreements get more popular, divorces get more common. I'd say that it's near 50% of marriages end in divorce. But I heard recently that this statistic includes second and third marriages which are more likely to get divorced than first marriage couples. Some say that the increase in popularity of divorce comes from women being more powerful and not afraid to leave their husbands. I think that's ridiculous but you can make the call.

I had lunch with my co-worker recently. Like most fathers, he talks about his kids a lot, especially his son as he plays little league. In this story, he told me that his wife got in a fight with another kid's father and his wife now forbids my co-worker to talk to the father outside of baseball. Previously, they were acquaintances, then he fought with his wife, now they're not. Just to clarify the situation, I asked him that if his wife didn't forbid him, would he still be friends with the guy, to which he replied, "Yes". In the situation, the guy realized that he was completely wrong in his issue with his wife and even if he didn't apologize, he could still move on knowing that the father knew he was wrong. He was just too narcissistic to admit it. Now you can see why people call marriage the last form of legalized slavery. Nobody has the right to tell you who you can and can't be friends with......not your spouse, not your parents, your priest, nobody! It appalls me that husbands always sit there and take it from their wives as they systematically control what they eat, drink, and do. Some husbands have curfews. This is absolutely ridiculous. I will not compromise my life for anybody, especially when it's only me making the compromises. This is why I can never get married, because that's the way the institution is set up. When it's not, it's the husband dominating the wife, which is actually more problematic than vice versa. Generally speaking, men are physically stronger than women, so if one side has the physical and mental control over the spouse, then that's problematic. The only way it works for the male to have control of both is if a religion has indoctrinated the female to accept this like devout Christians and Muslims do.

To further this point, I will talk about a fundamental flaw when woman and men talk to each other. A man cannot beat a woman in an argument because men are handicapped because they need to make sense in their arguments and will tend to stick to the issue. If you're male, you have many examples of this if you've ever argued with a woman. To give but one example, my family and I were in Venice at dinner. My mom got really mad at my dad for some reason. To this day, neither me, nor the other four members at the table (my dad and three siblings) have any idea why my mom was mad. At first my dad tried to find out what was wrong, but eventually realized how fruitless it was because my mom wasn't making any rational sense whatsoever. Finally, my dad just turned to my mom and said, "Honey, whatever I did to offend you, I'm sorry."

My mom responded, "It's okay," and immediately forgot about it.

I was 14 years old when this happened. I only remember that because we were in France before going to Italy and it happened when France won the world cup, which was 1998, making me 14. In any sane world, my dad's response should have failed miserably. If someone said that to me, I wouldn't feel better. Then again, I've never put someone in that situation because although I don't speak clearly, I do always manage to clearly articulate to someone why I'm pissed off at them. This shouldn't be difficult. You're mad at someone, this is why. Why can't women do this? Furthermore, how come we are automatically wrong when women just decide to yell incoherently? This just isn't fair to us men. Later, my dad relayed this story to his first cousin, to which he said that he did that to his wife all the time. Both he and my dad were proud of themselves for figuring out this trick. It's not a trick. It's just a ridiculous form of subjectivity they volunteered themselves into. Men don't even have a choice in how much to spend on the ring for their spouse. Convention clearly defines a three month's salary diamond ring. Why would men voluntarily decide to make so many concessions just to have a wife? I refuse to believe their quality of life is better. This is why when Louis CK said, "I don't want to hear single people complain to me, if you're single, you have absolutely nothing to complain about so I don't want to hear it." I agree.

I have a couple answers to the question why men decide to get married given everything I've said. One, they don't want to be alone for the rest of their lives. They have a fear of dying and nobody being at their side. This is very similar to my second point in that they want kids, and a wife increases your chances of having kids. Sometimes it happens the other way around in that you're having a kid, therefore you get married. Women use this as a tool to make men submit to marriage, a very underhanded tool if I must say. In fact, if you're a guy and this trick is being put on you, I'd demand a paternity test. When she bitches about her not trusting you, just tell her to add it to the tab of signing a prenuptial agreement. All joking aside, a lot of men want someone to carry on their name, or at least their DNA. They don't want to be the last one in their family line. Or, if they have brothers, the last of their unique traits. Well, it's a heavy cost, but if having your traits and genes passed on to the next generation is worth the remainder of your life as a slave with no real control over your life then so be it. A third reason is simply they don't want to lose the girl. Basically, the woman is pressuring, they've delayed it as long as they can so it comes between slavery or going back to the dating pool. They realize that maybe they're getting too old to go back to square one or they just hate the game or they believe they will never find someone better so they just give up trying. These are the main three reasons men get married. As for me, one of the reasons I don't want to get married is because I don't want kids and having a wife increases the possibility of that happening. Ironically, the reason men use to get married is one of the reasons I don't want to get married. I have two brothers to carry on the family name. I do not care about passing on my genes to the next generation and I quit playing the game four years ago and see no reason to go back. I also like being alone and do not care if nobody is at my side when I leave this world. This is why one of the best things that ever happened to me is the girl I fell in love with married someone else. Logically there was no way this girl was right for me for a variety of reasons but I believe she could have gotten me to submit. After all, relationships are never logical and I don't like things that aren't logical.

I've hinted at it and now I'm going to explain what my problem with kids is. All kids grow up and yell at their parents and probably even call them names like "Asshole." Think about everything your parents did for you. Now, if you were abandoned by your parents, I mean the person or people that raised you. To steal from one of my majors, economics, I'll just make a ridiculous assumption in order to simplify the world. My assumption is that the person who raised you from infancy to adulthood was your parent. I can say that everyone was raised by someone because I know how absolutely helpless we are as babies. Look at other species. Deer can walk minutes after birth, turtles know how to swim to the sea and raise themselves without their parents' presence, fish know how to swim downstream, and what about humans? We can't even figure out how to pick our heads up to breathe if we're lying face down. If someone picks us up shortly after birth, we could die if they don't know to support the head. No other species gets anywhere near the complete helplessness of humans after birth. The fact that guys like Locke can argue that there is no such thing as innate knowledge is testament to this. Now, your parent has taken you as this pathetically helpless creature that poops and cries all the time and nurtured you until you finally could start doing stuff on your own. And what do you do? Call your parents assholes… fuck you. Now, despite my view on this, I find my mom can frustrate and annoy me more than any person on the planet. I don't call her names because I do love my mom, but I think this love is why she can get under my skin the way she does. My mom is the only person I met that can convince me of something just by repeating it over and over again until I go brain dead and just believe it. Chris Rock says all women have this power, but I've only seen my mom utilize it effectively against me. All kids get frustrated by their parents, my point is… know your role and shut your mouth because the person that's frustrating you saved your life. For the better part of three years, you were a helpless pathetic creature and the frustrating person made sure you didn't die with absolutely no help from you. Cut the person some slack. Kids do not understand this, and I hold it against them.

Kids are also annoying and you're not allowed to tell them just how stupid they are. I addressed this in the chapter about "Conversations with My Kosta." Little kids start a sentence with, "Guess what…." And go on and on about God knows what and when they pause you say, "That's great."

Bullshit, it's not great. Tell your kid to tell stories that are actually interesting to the audience. Teach them the first rule to every speech is to know your audience. We do not care about how you saw Santa Claus' foot one time four years ago because we have some information on that subject that proves you're lying. Also, I have a problem when they draw you a picture and they have to tell you what it is and you look at it and have absolutely no idea what it is and you have to tell that kid, "Good job."

I do not like lying. If I tell the kid, "Good job," I am lying. The kid did not do a good job, in fact, it sucks. This is why I don't like modern art. I should not have to be told what you were drawing or painting, it should be quite obvious and if it's not, you suck. Sorry Picasso.

People who have seen me around little kids always say, "How can you hate them, when you're so good with them?"

The fact that I'm good with little kids is why I feel I can say I hate them. It's not that they don't like me. The other thing about having children is it signals the end of so many things. First off, you can never pack lightly ever again. I just went on an 18 day European vacation with nothing but a back pack. Not a traveler's back pack but something that a high school student would take to school with them. It has four pockets that get progressively smaller. I was able to fit everything I needed and even returned with some souvenirs. This is because I do not need much to survive. I've moved on with the help of my parents from the pathetic helpless creature to someone who can adapt and understands the bare essentials, which can fit in a backpack. I have learned this skill because I hate having a big suitcase. When a baby is introduced, a simple weekend trip demands pack and play, bassinet, diapers, blankets, etc. etc. You can never pack light until it grows up to not be so helpless and dependent. Secondly, to expand the first point, you really can't travel as much when you have a kid. Couples who argue in the beginning not to have children sometimes give the reason that they want to be able to go to Paris on a moment's notice and they can't do that with kids. They normally give in when they realize that they never have gone to Paris on a moment's notice. Well, I'm happy to report that I do not talk about traveling on a moment's notice, I do it. Therefore, it is a legitimate thing I would have to give up if I had children. In my 25 years, I've been to 23 countries. That's almost a new country every year of my existence. Not having the freedom to travel whenever I'm not burdened by financial or vacation days at work would be disastrous for me since I love to travel.

Thirdly, you have to plan everything when you have a kid. I'm not much of a planner. I live life spur of the moment. I just went back to Cleveland to surprise my mom for her birthday. Since I was only there for a day, I tried to see as many people as I could. When I called my friend who had a kid with his wife two months ago, he and his wife both gave me the same speech about how I need to give them notice because they just can't have me at their house without planning it around the babies' sleep schedule. My friend straight up told me everything had to be planned, even a trip to the McDonald's drive-thru. I don't want every moment of my life planned. Therefore, I do not want kids.

Another reason I don't approve of children is theoretically you love your wife. In fact, this is my next ridiculous assumption. All married couples with children love each other. Again, I apologize. The economics background forces me to make assumptions to simplify the world to make my point. Anyway, you love your wife and you have a kid. What you've just done is introduced another person that your wife loves more than she loves you. To be fair, I've heard fathers say that although they would get beaten up pretty badly for their wives, they would die for their children. Although I argue that I'd rather be dead than beaten to paralysis, which would be pretty bad. Their meaning was that they love their kids more than their wives. I just don't want that competition. Oedipus and Elektra complexes are real. If I had a wife, I probably had to beat out a lot of guys to get my wife, and I'll be damned if I create something in which I have no chance of beating for my wife's love. These are some of the reasons why when I hear someone tell me they just had a kid, I treat them like a child by saying "Congratulations. "The truth is that I feel really sorry for them that their life is over.

Now that I have given you some of the reasons why I don't want to get married with kids, I feel it is only fair to give you some problems I've encountered with this theory. One, men really do look happy on their wedding days. I don't understand it, but they do. It's indisputable. I have been to many weddings and despite the guy looking happy, I always attributed it to brain washing from the wife into accepting his enslavement. About a year ago, however, my friend got married to his long time girlfriend. I was a groomsman at the wedding and for the first time since I formed my views on marriage, I did not feel bad for the groom. In fact, their getting married made complete sense to the point that it didn't seem logical for them not to get married. I loved being a part of the wedding because I absolutely loved the bride for my friend. All grooms look happy at the church, but at the reception, you just saw a glow come over him and his wife. The day after the wedding, my friend's parents set up a buffet breakfast that I attended, and I saw my friend and his wife look calm and at peace. It's hard to explain but it seemed they were incomplete before and now they were whole. I don't normally talk like this, but if you were there, you'd probably have seen it too. Nobody wanted to leave this wedding. The best man, whose girlfriend was bitching that she wanted to leave early, put his girlfriend in his car to sleep while he went back in for a couple more hours. Keep in mind this is an October wedding in Cleveland, Ohio. Pretty cold.

She had the keys to turn on the car to stay warm but men just simply don't do that to their girlfriend's because they fear the repercussions. But he did because this was not a wedding you wanted to leave. As I looked at my friend glowing like I've never seen anyone glow before, I began thinking, "It would be really nice to find a girl that made me look like that."

I immediately became afraid because now I've opened the possibility of getting married. I write this off now as a moment of insanity and hope never to find a girl to make me look like that because it would go against everything I want in life.

Just in case this wedding wasn't already attacking some long held beliefs of mine, they had to attack the kids part too. Don't misunderstand, the bride is a devout Catholic and saved sex for marriage. One of her bridesmaids, however, was married with two children. She had been married to her husband, who was a groomsman, for four years. They had a four year old son and a baby. At the rehearsal dinner, both kids were in attendance. I was sitting across from the mother and our side of the table was engaged in a conversation. The baby was sleeping in his bassinet, and the four year old was on her lap and she was playing with him while talking with us. Then the baby woke up, she told the husband to get a chair. She then put the 4-year-old in the chair, picked up the baby and started feeding him with a spoon. I use the male pronoun because I feel bad using "it." Truth is, I do not remember if the baby was a boy or a girl. She did all this in smooth movements not missing the conversation. The four year old became interested in the knife in his arms reach, but every time he reached it, she gave him a stern look to put it down. In fact, the four-year-old never did any mischief without her noticing. She did all this while feeding the baby. Later, when she had to breast feed, she grabbed a blanket, covered herself, began breast feeding, while eating her food, keeping an eye on the four year old and having a conversation with us. Just thinking and witnessing everything she was doing simultaneously made me exhausted. I stared in amazement and focused closely on her face trying to find some ounce of frustration, exhaustion, or annoyance. She was doing all this seemingly effortlessly, as if she was born to do nothing else but be a mother. I relayed this to my mother and she told me that it's something you just do and was happy to see that she took to it so well as she assured me some women don't. I studied her hard but I saw absolutely no indication of fatigue, exhaustion, annoyance or frustration. I saw absolutely nothing that would confirm my belief that it is an unfortunate thing when you're married with children as young as she was. Finally, I just couldn't help myself and I just blurted out, "You are the greatest multi-tasker I've ever seen."

Immediately my friend's sister, who was seated near me, expressed her agreement as she was just as shocked as I was by what we were witnessing. The mother shrugged her shoulders as if to say, "What else am I supposed to?"

I left that wedding weekend with major chinks in my anti-wedding and anti-kids armor. It would be rebuilt later but I've included it because I want to be fair in my attacks and criticisms by revealing what I've discovered as valid points on the other side.

Before I get to my points on how to have a good marriage, let me just give one piece of advice on relationships: Make sure there's no ambiguity. This is more of a problem with women, but men do it too. Sometimes women think that they're dating a guy just because they hooked up after already knowing each other. This is simply not the case. There's a pretty easy way around this......... Ask the person. Since I'm old-fashioned, I will say that if you're a guy, ask the girl out. Say the words, "Do you want to go out with me?" If she says "Yes," good it's official. If she says, "When?" Clearly she misunderstood you so make it more obvious and say, "Do you want to be boyfriend and girlfriend?" It seems childish, and in a way it is, but it's the best and I would argue the only way to clear the ambiguity. If you start introducing him as your girlfriend (you can figure out how to reverse the sexes, it still applies), then the other person may be intimidated to call you out in public that you're not, so just ask him. If you're a girl, say to the guy, "Are we dating?" See what he says. Of course, the person can lie, but if they say, "Yes," then you can hold them to the list you made. I will describe the list shortly. Just as how you're not engaged until you ask your girlfriend, "Will you marry me?" with the ring and she says, "Yes." You're not dating unless you ask, "Do you want to go out with me?" and she says, "Yes."

In order to have a good marriage here's a list of things to follow. I will tell you now that it is very difficult to follow them but if you do, you will exponentially increase your chances of only getting married once and having it last a lifetime. (1) Make sure your parents (person who raised you) and closest friends approve (2) Make a list of unforgivable things and make sure you have never forgiven your significant other for doing them (3) Don't believe you will change who they are; you will fail and (4) You understand the meaning of the terms love and trust and you have both for your significant other, (5) Make sure you enjoy each other's company.

The first point is actually the most controversial. Most people say, "I don't let my parents pick my clothes, let alone my spouse."

Those people normally get divorced. Here's the sad fact, when you're in a relationship, you are the worst judge of how your relationship is. The reason being is you are completely blinded by your emotions. Even after my grandparents gave their blessings for my parents to get married, they still broke up, tried dating other people to see if they were just blinded by emotion before realizing that other relationships left them empty so they came back to each other. Think back of all your past significant others that you claimed you were in love with. How often were you wrong? The ones you admit you were wrong about, how many people close to you told you that you were wrong? What was your reaction? You probably yelled at them and said shit like, "You don't know him/her like I do." "You don't understand…." Or some bullshit like that.

Bottom line is, you don't understand. Your parents/friends can pick your spouse better than you can. This is why I'm not against arranged marriages since they didn't end in divorce nearly as often as marriages nowadays do. Since the practice of arranged marriages is pretty much dead, my compromise is for parents and close friends to approve. People always counter my mentioning the success rate of arranged marriages with how that in the times of arranged marriages, there weren't many divorces with it's because they were ashamed/scared to get divorced and that's why. Now it's okay to get divorced. I would say that if this were true, murderers of spouses and suicide would have been a lot more common. You may convince the entire world you're someone else, but you never fully convince yourself and you will act out and do outrageous things. Hence number three. Your parents, being older and have presumably gone through marriage, can better judge it than you can. Even if they're divorced, they can see if you're making the same mistakes they did. Please just listen. If you won't listen to them, close friends are the best alternative because they are also close to you and can see your relationship from the outside and be more objective. Their flaw is they usually haven't been married or experience what your parents have in this department.

Secondly, make a list of unforgivable things and make sure it hasn't been broken. Too often in today's society people base their morality on their or other people's actions rather than basing their actions on their morality. This is why you should physically write down the list. I understand emotions are completely irrational and making a list inserts objectivity to it, but you need to try to objectify it any way you can. When you have it in writing, it allows you not to convince yourself that it's not important. Do not make exceptions. Be stubborn. Do not be subjective. My list says I will not tolerate cheating and I will not tolerate someone having a definition of cheating different than my own. My definition is anything I wouldn't do with my sister or wouldn't want my sister doing to me. I've heard my friend say they would never tolerate cheating. Then the person she was with cheated multiple times and even got another girlfriend and wanted to just fuck her on the side and she was okay with it. When the new girl found out about her, she dumped him and my friend was the last girl standing and she was happy with it. During this time, she cheated on him multiple times to fill the void. By the way, promiscuity in both males and females is an indication of low self-worth. After a couple years, she stopped cheating and believed he did as well. She then justified the first couple of years as, "I didn't really know him and we weren't really dating." My rebuttal, you shouldn't have called him "boyfriend" for all these years then. This is where the fifth point comes in. She also changed her definition of cheating based on what he did. She still says she doesn't tolerate cheating but has proven that if he cheats, then she can just claim she didn't know him but now she does…until he cheats again that is. Make your list and stick to it. If you make a change, only do so when single.

Don't think you'll change them. This is truer for women than for men. People do not change. Yes, you can make them dress better, you can make them pay attention to hygiene and put the toilet seat back down, but you will not make a violent man non-violent, a womanizer monogamous or an asshole a nice guy. It will not happen despite your delusions to the contrary. The example you're thinking in your head is wrong, I guarantee it. There really isn't much more to say on this topic, it's pretty straight forward. It is true that when you first meet someone, they almost always put on a persona but after a couple months, the true nature comes out.

You need to understand the term love and trust. I will define them for you. Love is easy, because one of the three most brilliant people I've ever heard speak (Chris Rock, Trey Parker and Matt Stone) put it most eloquently, so I will steal his quote. Chris Rock said, "If you've never stood there with a bottle of rat poison in your hand and the only thing that stopped you from killing her was an episode of CSI, you've never been in love."

In my Catholic Jesuit high school when they wanted to be more specific than, "God is love" they said, "You don't think your significant other is perfect, instead you see the flaws and accept them as part of her and it doesn't bother you because of the feeling, you get." That's only half of it. You need to feel passion to be in love and the passion needs to be from both directions. I am not a sensitive person. In fact, I claim to be emotionally dead but the woman I fell in love with could piss me off more effortlessly and easily than any person I have ever met. Even when I asked myself what I would have done if another close female friend did the same thing, I could tell you that I wouldn't have cared in the slightest. But when she did it, I wanted to kill her. I very often got the urge to strangle her but something would always stop me. It may have been love. Or, the most severe beating from my father was when I hit my sister so I generalized to never hit a woman. A good lesson to learn by the way, and an excellent tool to instill it. Fuck you psychologist that doesn't agree. For whatever reason, I've known this girl for seven years now, and have never, and can confidently say will never hit her. If you don't have this passion, you're not really in love. People try telling me that they wouldn't care if Angelina Jolie straddled them, they wouldn't do anything because of what they feel for (insert girl's name here.)" I respond to this by saying they are lying and even if they weren't, that's still not love. You need to get the rage over little things they do just as you get so happy by their slightest touch. The 80's song, "Everything she does is Magic" needs to be there, but again, that's only the half of it. You need to also have the, "Every little thing she does pisses me off." Is it a contradiction because in this case neither is *everything?* Yes, but like I said, love is not rational at all. If you're ever indifferent to an action of your spouse, you're not in love. You need intense emotions to everything they do either way. Then you know you're in love.

As for trust, I can't speak too much about it because I do not trust anybody. Here's my test though...... If you think about signing a prenuptial agreement, you don't trust your significant other. That simple, if you trust them, it shouldn't and wouldn't even cross your mind.

Lastly, make sure you enjoy each other's company. If you can't talk to your significant other, don't get married. I understand men are not the best communicators or conversationalists but they are when they're with someone whose company they enjoy. Women can talk to anybody for hours. One of my closest friends cannot talk to anybody for more than 10 minutes except me and his current girlfriend. If you're not me or his girlfriend, you would make the excuse, "Well, he's just not much of a communicator." And you would be right. However, the exception to this is the bad communicator with the girl he loves. If you have a problem talking with your boyfriend, do not get married. If you think you enjoy your significant other's company then you should move in with them for a while and test it. I'm sorry Christians but this is the best way to see if marriage is right for you. When you live together you simply get to see all sides and angles that you cannot get any other way. It goes back to the fact that nobody changes. If the person is putting on a persona, they can't keep it up near 24 hours a day. Live together for at least a year. If you can't stand them it's a good thing you found that out before you got married.

Little Kids and How We Raise Them

Although I got into this in the previous chapter, I want to highlight my take on little kids. Keep in mind that this is being written by someone who self-proclaims himself to hate little kids. With that said, the way they are treated in this country is just plain wrong. I will start with the worst of the worst: Teachers. In my youth, whenever I met a teacher, I had the same reaction that society demands of me by saying, "Wow, you have a lot of patience. I can't deal with one little kid, let alone a classroom full of them."

As I grew older, I realized that I was talking about the teachers I had when I went to school rather than this new breed who, as far as I can tell, *really* hates little kids. As much as I hate to agree with Michael Moore, if you tell me that your 5-year-old likes running around, daydreams while sitting in school and can't focus on reading *War in Peace* for hours at a time........So you put him on a whole cupboard full of powerful psychiatric medication so he sits in the corner and stares straight for a while....... I will say you're a horrible human being. Let me tell you something about little kids. They run around, daydream and don't like spending their entire day reading. This is completely natural for a little kid. This is what they do, and it should be encouraged. Unfortunately, the days where I would get on my bike and ride around the neighborhood and my parents said nothing so long as I was home before dinner is over because of pedophiles. But kids should still be encouraged to play.

Parents normally do a good job of that until they send their kids to school. Then the teacher is impatient and gets frustrated with kids acting like kids, so they convince the parents that their kids have a psychological disorder and need a powerful drug cocktail to get rid of it. To put the cherry on their self-centered, I hate my job so I'm going to take it out on as many people as I possibly can whining, they will call Children's Services to take your kid away from you if you refuse. If you don't believe me, there was a case where a woman pulled her kid out of school, the authorities stole her child, she went into the facility, stole her kid back, fled California to Canada, the authorities followed her into Canada and took the kid back. As a point of reference, police officers don't follow murderers and drug traffickers into other countries for an arrest. But Children's Services does.

I urge you parents to have faith that you know your child better than his or her teacher. Please don't let anybody convince you otherwise. If you're one of these parents that believe that the teacher is right because "After many months of my kid taking a cupboard full of anti-psychotic medication, I took him off it and he became completely rambunctious and violent so I had to put him back on." I want to do to you what you should do to your child... spank you! I'm sorry, but hitting your kids as a form of discipline isn't only healthy, it's really the only way they learn. Kids do not learn by being yelled at, they will ignore it. Every lesson I've learned was beaten into me. Now, if you beat your kids for no reason, that's despicable. There needs to be a reason and if you leave bruises or have to hospitalize them, then clearly you've gone too far. Like the saying goes, "Everything in moderation." So that's how you deal with unruly kids. Now to point out the obvious, your kid is going through something very common with drugs, it's called withdrawal.

My closest friend right now, who is one of the least sensitive people I know, became absolutely enraged and viewed it as a fighting act when I took ONE of his cigarettes and broke it. Not a pack, but one. And that's a cigarette, which isn't nearly as strong as any psychiatric drugs, let alone the cocktail you're giving your kid. So, deal with the withdrawal because you're the fucking dumbass that gave him all the drugs in the first place.

Now, if you're a teacher that doesn't recommend parents to drug their kids to make your job easier, clearly I'm not talking about you. Unfortunately, you're a minority. Also, my parents were always bothered by the fact that despite my dad being a highly respected and decorated ophthalmologist, they found out that all four of their kids needed glasses because our teachers told them. This doesn't mean your teachers know your children better than you, it means that the teacher, who writes things on the board and then asks your child to read it, tests vision regularly whereas you don't. Despite my dad's knowledge of eyes, he can't look into my eyes and see whether or not I can see far; still need an eye test for that one. Eyesight has nothing to do with personality. You know the personality of your child better than your teacher and let nobody tell you otherwise.

I was extremely lucky to have parents that were always on my side. Some teachers tried to tell my parents about what type of kid I was. One even got me tested for ADD. To date, I'm the only kid I know that failed that test. By failed, I mean that I was tested and they determined that I did not have ADD. Every other kid I know tested was shown to have ADD because they acted like a kid. I, however, actually always enjoyed reading. I also think that the test is more conducive to positives than when I was 10 years old.

Back to the original point, kids need to know that their parents are on their side because if they don't, they feel helpless and withdraw, which is never good. If your children aren't comfortable to be themselves in their home, then where can they be? I wish parents understood this but the more I see parents accepting a teacher telling them how their kids are and automatically discrediting them, I can't help but think that I am one of the few whose parents were always on my side. I will give a couple examples of the contrary just to give you examples to make sure you're not doing this to your child.

When I was at an amusement park, I was waiting in line for a ride and this little girl started skipping up to the person in front who had just moved up. While skipping her foot hit the railing and she tripped and fell. Her mother turned to the mother of a little kid who was on the other side of the railing and said, "Your kid just tripped mine, thanks a lot." The mother turned to her kid and said his name as if to scold him.

Since I was further back in line as to be on the other side of the railing as the accused boy, I was also in ear shot of the mother. I snapped, "No, don't yell at him, he didn't do anything, the girl kicked the railing and fell."

Another woman from further back actually cut the line to tell the mother the same thing then retreated because she heard me, said a quick confirmation that I was right, and went back. The mother turned to me and said, "Okay, but he would do something like that."

Your child should not hear this. You just admitted to a complete stranger, in front of your child, that if I wasn't there, you freely would have blamed him because of something a stranger accused him of and you wouldn't have believed him if he protested. I feel bad for that kid. I know little kids are irrational and they talk way too much, but if you accuse them of something at least hear what they have to say. Yes, little kids, like most human beings, will lie to save themselves from getting in trouble, but at least give them a chance.

Another example is this 12-year-old I knew well because he was very close with my family. He was an extremely good soccer player, and many coaches of other teams would go up to his father to try to convince him to play for their team. When I talked to him about this, he was very humble and modest about it. Most kids that excel well in sports are arrogant about it, however, he never let all the attention get to his head. I complemented his father about this. His father told me, "Yea well that's his problem, he never listens to anybody and nothing gets through to that boy's head, so it's actually not a good thing."

I protested to no avail. The father refused to believe me that it was a good thing that his son wasn't arrogant about his soccer ability. I have extreme respect for the father, but given that debating with him was a losing battle, I focused my energy to the 12-year-old. I encouraged him to not become arrogant and tried to guide him when he would act out in school or do other things his father justifiably wouldn't approve of. Predictably, he was scared of his father and had the idea that nothing he ever did would be right. In psychology, this is called "learned helplessness" in that kids are taught that nothing they do will better their situation, so they stop trying. I frequently forced him to talk to me about his problem with his dad and convinced him that he was wrong in thinking that his father viewed everything he did as bad intentioned or wrong. I succeeded very well, and as I've watched the kid grow up, he doesn't seem to have the signs of learned helplessness that I saw when he was 12. I will not give myself credit for this, but I know I tried to get this result.

For those of you that suspect that I lied to him about his father, you're wrong. If you proceed to think I'm contradicting myself since I prefaced the story by saying his father did do that, I will explain what I did. I used fancy rhetoric in order to not make any fallacious statements, but make it seem like they contributed to the point that his father didn't believe he was guilty until proven innocent even though they didn't. I do not like using fancy rhetoric, but when I'm in a situation where I really don't want to be truthful, I resort to it because it's a lesser of two evils (lying or fancy rhetoric). As I write this, I'm pained to imagine what would have happened to him if he didn't have influences to counteract his father in his life. Since I didn't see him very often, I doubt I was the only one, but I am the only one I know of. A fact that parents hate to hear is that they are not the greatest influences in their kid's lives, their peers are. This fact may have saved the kid.

Fast forwarding, when he got older and was in a position to rebel, he called me for advice. Although he scolded me for having views more strict than his father, he did listen. The mere fact that he called me for my advice makes me believe that I influenced him.

The final example I will give is similar to the last one. I went on a family trip with my friend's family. He had a brother that was at least four years younger than me. I was graduating high school that year and he was going to be a freshman the following year. As I wandered around, I walked in on a conversation between him and his father on a balcony.

Before I get into the conversation, I will say that this kid was the smartest person I have ever met younger than me. He certainly was smarter than me at that age. His ability to grasp concepts, and then logically apply them to other areas was unprecedented. He had limitless potential if he set his mind to it. His father knew this too, which you may think is a good thing. Except for the fact that his father didn't want any of his kids to outperform him, this kid was the biggest threat.

As I went out on the balcony, I overheard his father say, "Why am I paying for you to go to a private Catholic Jesuit School."

"To get a good education."

"Yea, well you're smart enough that you could figure out a way to succeed in a public school. You're older brother (my friend) needed the good institution because he needs the name school as a crutch to help him get into a good college, but you could figure your way to the top even at a public school. Seems like a waste of money to me."

"I don't know dad."

I couldn't listen to this anymore as I saw him retreating and being intimidated. I jumped in and explained how kids should be given every opportunity to succeed. The father could easily afford sending the kid to the Catholic Jesuit School and given how he could succeed at a public school, imagine what he could do at a college preparatory school? He stayed silent as I took over the argument with the father. Many people will condemn me for getting involved, but I had become close enough with this family that I looked at this kid like a younger brother. Actually, I treated him more like a little brother than my own younger brother. I had to defend him.

As you can see from some of these stories, I stick my nose where it doesn't belong a lot, but I just can't deal with injustices. I may hate little kids, but they need no help from their parents to be terrors. If I see a parent helping the process, I speak up. I urge you, if you're going to have kids, be supportive of them. Compliment them when they succeed. You don't have to reward mediocrity or failure, but don't stand in their way of achieving their potential. The more of a threat you become, the more likely they may shoot up a school or become just another juvenile delinquent in our society, and we don't need any more of those.

Other problems I have in the way people raise their kids comes in the form of "play dates." Kids should not be scheduled to play, it should naturally occur. A little kid, when left alone, will play. At work, a woman who has young children said to another guy who had kids of similar age, "We should arrange for our kids to have a play date."

I kept my mouth shut as I hate this term and try to keep my views private at work. Luckily, the guy had the same views I did, he threw up his arm and said, "No, we will not be making any appointments, someone is always home, come over any time you want with your kids and they will start playing. I don't do play dates, you and your kids are always welcome, so come by whenever you want."

The woman continually tried to justify her position to no avail. The guy was adamant, "There's always someone home, come over whenever you want, no need to plan anything." That's how it was done when I was a child, and I would love to see the tradition continue.

Aren't kids annoying when they're running around and being obnoxious? Little kids have more stamina than adults, and it's exhausting playing with them because they want to keep going. It's like petting a dog. The dog will always want to be petted longer than you are willing to pet it. I will admit, if all the kids were drugged to not run around, I would have less of a problem with them. It would be beneficial to me because I don't like little kids simply because they act like little kids. Unfortunately for me, I was taught in the ways of economics. Economics teaches us that if there's a program that helps more people than it hurts, you should do it. Conversely, if the plan harms more people than it helps, you shouldn't. In this situation, stifling kids by meaningless structure like play dates or drugs hurts all little kids and helps the group of people who dislike little kids. I don't have an exact number, but I guarantee you that there are more little kids than there are people who don't like little kids. Also, if you factor in that kids on powerful drugs may become violent during withdrawal may shoot or harm others, it seems indisputable that the current policy of stifling children, hurts more people than it helps. Despite my being in the latter group, it's a bad strategy, stick to the letting kids use their imaginations and play and discipline them when they get out of line without using drugs.

MAKING THE PERFECT THE ENEMY OF THE GOOD.

Making the perfect the enemy of the good is a bastardization of a saying created by Morton Blackwell. He has a number of points that he advises those he employs at his company, The Leadership Institute. One of these points is, "Don't make the perfect the enemy of the good." Not many people know of the Leadership Institute so I will briefly describe my former employer knowing full well that they could probably help me promote this book and this chapter may destroy that. The only important thing about Morton Blackwell that you far-left people should know is that when Hillary Clinton made her web of the "Vast Right Wing Conspiracy, which is eerily similar to *The Protocals of the Learned Elders of Zion,* Morton Blackwell was in the middle of the web. The Leadership Institute is a conservative organization that tries to get conservatives into the public forum in order to not indoctrinate the public with solely leftist points of view as it is now with TV and newspaper. I accepted an offer with the Leadership Institute because I believed this to be a worthy cause. I was also desperate for a job since my parents, who decided to give New York a shot, had just re-confirmed that they didn't like living in New York so moved back to Cleveland. And since I was no longer in college, I'd have to follow them if I didn't think of something. Consequently, I took the job with the Leadership Institute so that I could be sent to Kentucky to work for them so that

I could pay for my Manhattan apartment. I still live in New York so as ridiculous as the plan was, it worked. I bought myself enough time till I found a job I enjoyed in New York. That's the Leadership Institute and my relation to it in a nutshell.

"Making the perfect the enemy of the good," means that because someone isn't as hardcore as you, you vilify them. I am extremely right wing when it comes to the general public. As it related to the Leadership Institute, I was moderate at best. To give an example, a vast majority of the people in the room said things like, "I'm against the war in Iraq... instead, we should be at war with Mexico because illegal immigration is the greatest problem we face so we should declare war on Mexico" and, "The Catholic Church is a liberal institution."

This is a little too right-wing for this humble author. I would be "Making the perfect the enemy of the good" if I were to attack conservatives that are more right wing than I and people such as Republicans who are to the left of me. Morton Blackwell compels conservatives not to do this and focuses attacks on the left wing fake victims who pretend that they are being oppressed when it is the opposite that is true. Well, Mr. Blackwell, this is my book and I will attack whoever the fuck I want.

Like its far-left counter parts, the Leadership Institute sounds good on paper but they contradict themselves. They are an extremely bureaucratic organization and they say they hate red tape. This big government bureaucracy does everything they can to inhibit business from succeeding too well. If you're against bureaucracy, don't be so bureaucratic. To be fair, perhaps when running a business you need to be bureaucratic.

Lehman Brothers was very lax with their workers and didn't make them go through red tape to work later or other things. Barclays Capital is extremely strict and very bureaucratic. Lehman Brothers failed in 2008 and Barclays survived. There is an entire list of other reasons this possibly happened and someone with a better knowledge of finance than I could probably tell you, but I point out this one difference. To bolster my point, if the American army wasn't so bureaucratic and didn't follow rules the enemy doesn't follow, we would have been allowed to invade Saigon during the Vietnam War and most likely saved thousands of lives by winning the war earlier. By comparison, imagine how much harder World War II would have been if General Patton wasn't allowed to march into Berlin. I'd argue bureaucracy has killed more American soldiers than any other factor.

But the bureaucracy isn't even the worse part. Morton Blackwell comes to talk with the new employees during a one week intense training for the job. We heard from a variety of speakers and one actually encouraged us to vote Democrat when there are weak Republican candidates (He put Bush Jr. in this category) because sometimes it is important to destroy the county so that the country shifts right and a real conservative Republican candidate can take over and fix everything making the country better off. He gives the example that if Jimmy Carter didn't screw up the country then Americans never would have elected Ronald Reagan. As I write this, I realize that my all time hero and person I agree with more than any other author, Ayn Rand, would probably agree with this assessment since her most famous book is pretty much exactly about this. I don't mention the name of the book in case you decide to read it. I don't want to spoil it for you. I didn't agree with this point and have no problem if moderates who lean right are leading the country because I think they'll do a better job than the Democrats. Destroying and rebuilding the country sounds dangerous to me. After he spoke, I approached Morton Blackwell and asked him if he truly believed this and if this was the policy of the Leadership Institute. Now, he could have said, "Well we try to give people as many different conservative views as we can, because different people will borrow from different aspects in forming their beliefs. If you don't believe this, that's your right."

I would have put pressure on him to see if he himself believed this since I am so against this point but that would have been a fine answer. I understand he doesn't want to "make the perfect the enemy of the good" and an outright condemnation would be doing that. But that's not what he did. He spoke for about a full minute and said absolutely nothing. I haven't seen someone dodge a question like that since Bill Clinton. I followed it up by saying, "I am a fundamental Objectivist who completely believes in the work of Ayn Rand. You claim Objectivists as conservatives in your list of different names, but I don't think that's fair, what do you think?" Again, he spoke at length and said absolutely nothing. This is the owner and leader of an organization that is supposed to be against these famous left wing strategies and, instead, exemplified them. Morton Blackwell, conservatives are supposed to take a stand, they're supposed to not bloviate and bullshit, they clearly define their position and wait for the attacks. You let your conservative followers down when you refuse to answer questions clearly.

Ann Coulter is another famous conservative writer. I love her books. Even the New York Times said something along the lines of a great deal of research goes into Miss Coulter's diatribes. If you've read any of her books and see how vehemently she attacks the New York Times, this is an amazing compliment. I actually see it as the New York Times waving the white flag and admitting they just can't beat her. That is until I read *Guilty*. Now, I admit I'm not as good a researcher as Ann Coulter. When I was in Kentucky, however, I was bored out of my mind, so I decided to research my only really liberal view. I'm pro-abortion. To see my view on this subject, see the chapter, which is very subtly called "Abortion." Ann Coulter's most controversial view in this book is when she attacks single mothers. She does a good job of explaining this and so to do her justice, I will clarify. She clearly defines a single mother as someone that got knocked up by a stranger or someone she had no intention of starting a family with but merely needed his sperm for a baby, has the baby and raises it by herself because she doesn't believe she needs a man to raise her baby. She calls single mothers that are single as a result of a divorce or widowed as a separate category. She quotes that eighty percent of the kids in Juvenile Hall were the result of single mothers. That's simply not true. I have done this research. Eighty percent of the kids in Juvenile Hall are adopted kids, which is why I do not like adoption and much prefer the abortion alternative. Ann Coulter used the rate of adoptive kids that are arrested before the age of eighteen, rather than the single mother statistic, which I do not know. No person that attacked Ann Coulter on this belief brought this up. I believe they just didn't know, and that proves that the left-wing doesn't believe in finding out the facts. I always believed they would seek out facts to dispute conservative giants like Ann Coulter, which is why I never decided to check Ann Coulter's copious references she makes in her book. I have heard a lot of people say, "Well, people have checked her references and found them to be mostly bullshit."

I always ask for an example of what she said that the reference was bullshit or name one person who did this study so I can read their work. I have never gotten a useful answer. All I get is, "Oh come on you can't possibly believe her bullshit" or "I don't know, you look it up," or some derivation of that. I'm now curious if Ann Coulter does make other stuff up since I know she lied about this. I hope this to be her only mistake, because I have huge respect for Ann Coulter and was very disappointed to read that chapter. Although I admit she's better at research than I am, even the book *Freakonomics* by Steven Levitt & Stephen Dubner found my statistics about adopted children.

Bill O'Reilly is someone I have a great deal of respect for but have a message for him as well. Here's one fact about Bill O'Reilly that I don't believe there is a better example of. He is hated by both the far-left and the far-right. He is attacked from both sides and that is why I believe him to be fair and balanced. It's not too difficult a concept to conceive of. O'Reilly seems to understand this point because he will do polls to prove it. For example, during the 2008 presidential election, as the election drew near he asked, "Do you think my coverage of the presidential race favored McCain, favored Obama or was equal?" If you think I'm going to say that a majority of people said it was equal, you're wrong. That wouldn't prove my point at all since the point was he is attacked by the right and left equally. The poll came back 40% said he favored McCain, 40% for Obama. I presume the final 20% said he was fair but I do not remember if he had a fourth category that said, "Not sure." An equal percentage of people thought he favored Obama and McCain, there is no better example of fair and balanced than that. Now, most people will make the following criticism of me without a doubt, but I wish O'Reilly would stick to things he actually knows what he's talking about.

Bill O'Reilly knows nothing about economics, and when he takes on an economic point of view he proves it again and again. Now, when people make these criticisms of O'Reilly in e-mails he always says, "That's nice, give me an example now."

Okay Bill I will. In fact, just for shits and giggles, I'll give you two. He had Ben Stein on the show arguing about how he believes oil speculators are driving up the price of oil. In the summer of 2009, an article in one of the left-wing propagandist treacherous mainstream newspapers I've longed boycotted reported on this story so Bill O'Reilly called victory but really just because a newspaper did an article on it, doesn't prove anything. Anyway, back to what happened. Ben Stein told Bill O'Reilly that there are a variety of factors that go into the price of oil; for instance, people's expectation. O'Reilly cut him off and said, "Oh now you're going to tell me that people's expectation has anything to do with the price of goods, that's absolutely ridiculous."

Well silly me, every single economic textbook that I had to read and studied in school had all these formulas that had P_e or C_e indicating People's expectation or Consumer expectation. I wonder why that is. Oh yea, I remember because it has a lot to do with it! I'll give you an analogy since you went to Harvard and every time I've heard a Harvard professor speak, it's been something completely idiotic so presumably your time there probably made you dumber since you were taught by morons. If the country was convinced that tomorrow the price of gas was going to raise by a dollar a gallon, what do you think would happen? See this is why I like economics, it's more about predicting people's reactions than predicting markets. I'll tell you what I would have done when I owned a car. I'd go to the gas pump today and fill it up. I'd imagine almost everyone who had regular access to a car would do the same. With everyone going to get gas today, the gas stations would have to deal with a huge demand. With a large increase in demand, and no change in supply, something happens…oh what did I learn in all those economics classes, oh yea, the price goes up. If enough people did believe it, yes it could increase by a dollar a gallon thus proving the source of whatever convinced the whole country that gas would raise by a dollar (yes as I've told you, making ridiculous assumptions is also something I learned as an economics major). This is why people or consumer's expectations affect price.

In the summer of 2008, gas prices sky rocketed. Bill O'Reilly had a field day with this because he got to cover his three year campaign against the oil industry. During the fall and winter, the price of gas dropped and people stopped trying to sell their cars and began driving again. I know during the summer of 2008, it was a lot harder to find parking when I had to move my car twice a week to avoid a ticket for street cleaning, which is known to people who own cars in New York City but can't afford garages or a residence with a driveway. Also during that summer, there were more cars that had for sale signs in their windows than I'd ever seen. With this seemingly decrease in demand, and the price of a barrel of oil decreasing, the price of gas did too. This wasn't good enough for O'Reilly, he pointed out that the percentage decrease in the price of gas was less than the percentage decrease in the price of a barrel of oil. By itself, I wasn't too alarmed, it's not always a direct proportion. I doubt that if the price of grain goes up, the price of a slice of pizza goes up in the same percentage. Just in case this little criticism isn't enough, I found out another fact by the guy he brought in on this point. The guy pointed out that in the summer of 2008 the percentage increase in the price of gas was less than the percentage increase in the price of a barrel of oil. So what you're telling me is that gas both fell and rose by a less percentage than the price of a barrel of oil. O'Reilly's response was that that was irrelevant. Bill, to steal a page out of your book, please explain how that fact is irrelevant? Oh wait, I know, it presents a legitimate, logical, and factual attack on your oil speculation theory, which is your baby and you are against anything that attacks your baby. In the objective, no-spin forum that you try to live in, you need to admit that your critique is wrong on both the price expectation doesn't affect price and it is not irrelevant if the price rises and falls by a similar percentage between two goods points. For the theory as a whole, I do not know if oil speculators unfairly manipulate the price of gas. Given the large difference in gas prices between Europe and America (Europe is measured in liters and if you do the conversion it's closer to six dollars for a gallon of gas in Europe), there might be something to that theory. Your baby that you've been fighting for over three years will not be destroyed if you make the concessions that 1) People or consumer expectations affect price of goods and 2) It is relevant that the price of gas increased at a lower percentage than the price of a barrel of oil in 2008. In the future, please pick up any economics book to get some basic knowledge about economics before commenting about economic issues. To be fair to Mr. O'Reilly, he did bring on Ben Stein and the other guy to debate with him so that the general viewer, like me, can decide who they think is right. This is why I love the *O'Reilly Factor*, he brings on people who disagree with them and let's the viewer decide. Most of the time the viewers are split on who they agree with as evidenced when he reads e-mails at the end of the show.

A broad criticism of people I respect is that they don't apply the same microscope to the other side of the argument. To give a vague example, nobody understood Dan Brown's real message in his famous books that religion and science can co-exist. The non-religious people said, "Yea, look at the church's lies." The religious people said, "He's godless." I will analyze this by repeating what I heard in my Catholic Jesuit School science classes. Science seeks to explain God's creations. The fact that everything is so neatly organized, all our cells work together in systems to form organs and other tasks and, despite our best ability to destroy them with foreign substances, they adapt to keep us alive and that one slight derivation means we're dead shows God. At the end of the book, *Angels and Demons* Dan Brown does an excellent job of revealing this point but when people talk about the book, they seem to ignore that part. Ann Coulter attacks Darwinism, without using the same microscope on Creationism. O'Reilly doesn't put his microscope on gas decrease that he does on gas increase. These people bother me more than the far-left because I don't believe the far-left is capable of thinking for themselves. The O'Reilly's and the Coulter's are, they just decide to shut it off for their crusades.

THE WORLD HASN'T PROGRESSED IN 5,000 YEARS

Well, I suppose there are some people who first became interested in this book by the title. Thankfully, I have it as one of the chapters. What could I possibly mean by this? We have computers, the internet, the I-phone$_{TM}$, Nintendo Wii$_{TM}$, people are living a lot longer than they did before, how can I say something like this? Well, because all the above things are superficial and surface things, we as a species are having the same debates that the ancient Greeks had.

Everything is objective, there is no subjectivity, there is always a right answer and a wrong answer. Most of you disagree with that statement. Most people that lived in ancient Greece disagreed with that statement. Maybe you can recognize some of the people that agree with that statement: Socrates, Aristotle, and Plato to name three. Socrates devoted his life to proving the Sophists wrong. He believed that the Sophists were the scum of society and their influence needed to be withered. Sophists were people who believed that there is no right or wrong answer, but if a position is argued with fancy enough rhetoric, anything can be true. Socrates said that you may be able to convince things of people but that doesn't make it right. The main problem Sophists have is they believe that people are the most important things on Earth and what they say goes. This is not the case. What do we say today? I've never heard of a group of people called Sophists so Hooray!

Socrates, Aristotle and Plato were right. Slow down, A) most of you disagreed with the previous point so at least in spirit they haven't won but what if these Sophists just decided to call themselves something else. Let's think of what they could be called, how about "Lobbyists." Like Sophists, Lobbyists were employed by people in power to convince the general public that what they were doing was right. Phillip Morris has doctors that have found that nicotine is not addicting and the Lobbyists point this out. They say things like, "It has never been definitively proven that nicotine is addicting."

They don't scream that too loudly now, but that is their point. They just spin the argument to make it easier to swallow for the public. Now corporations and government officials use Lobbyists to argue with other Lobbyists to try to put their views into law or stop others from being law. This is what the Sophists did too and those of us who try to oppose them are picking up the fight for Socrates. If you think only the anti-Sophists have famous names on their side, you are sorely mistaken. Nietzche, Kant, Sartre, and pretty much the entire existentialist movement were all descendents and promoters of Sophistry. In order for me to call it a progression, the debate should be how Plato fought with Aristotle. Plato said that it is impossible for human beings to reach the objective truth in a matter, but that is not a reason to not strive for it. For if we strive for it, we will get closer to it than by any other means. Their method of getting there is by arguing. Aristotle believed that we could achieve the objective truths. They didn't use this terminology. Plato called objective truths, "The Forms." We don't know what Socrates called them because he never wrote anything down. Instead, Plato took what he learned and wrote it down for him. If you have a problem with this, you must also have a problem with Darwin and Jesus, since their famous words were written by other people. The general public still rejects objective truths. Some will give the famous moderation theory in that some things are objective truth, some are not. I disagree, but I go into that in the "Objectivism" chapter. I would call it progress if today's debates pitted Aristotle followers against Plato's followers. If that were true, the world would be a better place because the general public would be smarter.

Yes, healthcare has progressed making people live longer. I just don't think it has as much as it seems. We still have yet to cure a virus whether it's the common cold or AIDS. I'm beginning to lose hope in this. This is why it's laughable when people say we haven't cured AIDS because it's a Gay or Black disease. AIDS is a virus, we haven't cured any viruses, so why would AIDS be an exception? People are horrified by middle ages therapies such as leeches, bloodletting and amputation. Have we really abandoned these methods? When infections are so severe that modern day antibiotics can't alleviate it, doctors resort to amputation or maggots. See...... maggots feed on rotting tissue, like infections, but not on healthy tissues. So, maggots do a very good job of literally consuming the infection, and the people in the middle ages realized this. Also, the best way to stop something from spreading is to localize it and amputate. Something we still do today. All we really did was eliminate the need for the drastic measures. In the old days, they took the last case scenario and applied it to everything. To put the analogy to war, they had a fatal weapon like a gun and used it to kill everything from flies to moose. Now, we have fly swatters to deal with the lesser things like flies but only when it's as big as moose do we resort to the heavy artillery. Is that really that much of a change?

Then if you look at what we do for cancer, you really need to ask yourself the same question. After chemotherapy, which is a devastating treatment in and of itself, we nuke the area you had cancer in. The theory is that if we kill everything, the healthy cells will grow back but the cancerous cells won't. One, don't they keep telling me that the radiation from cell phones and my microwave will cause cancer, how can the prevention be the exact same thing? Well, maybe radiation in moderation is harmful but extreme radiation is good. Even if that's true, you can't tell me that this is more humane, and less barbaric than having maggots eat dead tissue leeches suck out whatever leeches sucked out and cutting you so that your body is forced to clean itself (which is what bleeding is) in order to defend the body against infection or further disease. Chemotherapy and radiation treatment is the best indication that healthcare hasn't come that far. Since I hate cancer more than any other disease since it killed my best friend at 18-years-old and my grandfather, I'm most appalled that we still resort to barbaric middle-aged treatment of this disease.

When people discover any proof of the fact the world hasn't progressed in 5,000 years, they resort to ridiculous explanation like aliens did it. We thought we were so cool when we discovered π for our circles and mathematics. Then we measured the pyramids in Egypt and found π. We then set out to build pyramids as big as the Egyptians using theirs as a model. We failed miserably! We even had the model and we couldn't do it. But we're so much smarter than they were right? How can we justify it? I know, we'll say, "Aliens did it."

Nice, and by nice I mean you're a moron. The Egyptians didn't have Nintendo, anti-psychotic and psychological drugs, *The New York Times*, MSNBC, BBC, NBC, CNN, and other methods that inhibit our ability to think and make us stupid. The Parthenon is the most geometrically sound building in the entire world. It was once used to store gun powder (thank you Turks) and then in a war with Italy, it was bombed. So a structure that was used to store gunpowder is bombed, and it's still standing afterwards? People will point out that the Parthenon is not perfectly intact as the pediment on top is gone, along with the roof and the painting on the inside. Also since 1985, they've done some renovations on it. My comeback, fill any other building with gunpowder and bomb it, see what happens. I hate to use this point of reference because I live in New York City and am eternally saddened by the events of September 11. Two modern day skyscrapers didn't fare too well when a plane hit them, and they were designed to withstand a plane crash from the biggest plane at the time. The World Trade Center was not filled with gunpowder when the planes hit it. The Parthenon was when it was bombed. I can visit the Parthenon today, I can't visit the World Trade Center because it is gone. I'm relieved that the steel from the World Trade Center was used to build a US Navy ship so that's what it is now. When it comes to building buildings that will last, the ancients seem to have us beat despite all the "advancements" in engineering.

Unless you are a little kid, I'm pretty sure you've thought or said something like, "When we were that age, we never did something like that." This is not a new theory. In Baldassare Castiglione's, *The Book of the Courtier*, Castiglione says this exact thing about the next generation. He does so in the context of people talking. Then one person points out the obvious. Since our parents say the same thing about our generation and their parents to them, this simply cannot be true because then we'd all be cannibalistic, immoral, unscrupulously pieces of trash and we wouldn't have been on this Earth as long as we have. The point is.... we find out what little kids are doing more now because when we were that age, we were more narrow minded and unable to see what was going on around us. I hear of 12-year-olds giving blow jobs and having sex and I respond, "We never did that shit." Yes we did. I just didn't. I have met people who lost their virginity at that age but when I was that age nobody told me they had just done that. This is true for every generation. People who lived in the 50's say things like, "We could keep our doors on our houses and cars unlocked and nothing would happen to them. Crime was a lot less rampant back in my day."

No, our methods of catching criminals was different, the crime remained the same. Also, there were times when we left our front door wide open, I even did in my apartment in Brooklyn at one point and left for a while. Nobody took anything. I also lived in a nice house that stood out to be robbed, but nobody robbed it. I'm not saying you should try this, I'm saying that maybe things haven't changed that much. We're just more fearful now. Eventually you have to stop using the excuse, "Well you just got lucky."

How come I don't get this lucky when I go to Atlantic City and Vegas? During the Renaissance, Castiglione revealed this problem and proved how illogical and stupid it was. His book was popular so many people had access to this information. Yet we still continually have the exact same discussion.

Before I begin my next example of this, I will say that I am Greek Orthodox. I believe in God. I don't like organized religion because I think Jesus' teachings don't need a translator, but I will always be Greek Orthodox because A) I think you should only convert if you believe that another religion has better answers than your current one and I think all organized religion is wrong. Therefore, a better one won't be found and B) Being Greek Orthodox isn't really exclusive from being Greek. Non-Greeks have converted to Greek-Orthodoxy and not all Greeks are Greek Orthodox but I wouldn't feel right calling myself Greek if I wasn't Greek Orthodox and being Greek is such a large part of who I am. Now, to get to my point.

What were the Greek myths? The world couldn't explain things therefore they created God or gods to explain them. They didn't understand the rotation of the Earth, so the Greeks said every morning Apollo used his chariot to bring the sun across the sky. Bill Maher does a good job in *Religious* talking about where beliefs about Jesus came from. Since Jesus appears in a variety of Muslim and non-Christian texts, sorry Bill Maher, Jesus the man existed. Now, was he God is a completely different question. Religion is just another name for a myth. Since we can't explain it, we say, "God did it." Sometimes we throw aliens into the mix like with the Egyptian pyramids.

One of the major "discoveries" in scientific history isn't even a progression. We still can't explain how creatures appeared on the Earth and how the different ones were created. Entire books are written on this topic, so I will just sum up what they found as best I can. Darwin said in *Origin of Species* that the fossil record will eventually prove or disprove his theory. We've had a lot of archaeological digs and found a lot of fossils since *Origin of Species* and the evidence is pointing toward disproving. Archaeopteryx was supposed to be the link between dinosaurs and birds. It looks like a half-bird half dinosaur. Everyone proclaimed this as a victory for Darwinists. Well, the earliest Archaeopteryx fossils were dated several thousands of years after the first birds appeared on Earth. It seemed to miss the big dinosaurs turning to birds explosion. How could the transitional species come after the end result? According to Darwin, it doesn't.

We can't explain the pre-Cambrian explosion either. One minute there weren't many multi-celled organisms then poof, all these more complex organisms started showing up. Scientists say that the terrain during that time didn't allow for fossilizations so all their ancestors just didn't fossilize. That's not very convincing. The eye is extremely complex with all its parts and connections to the brain, but how it came to be, fossils can't tell us. Darwin said only the strong survive. So where are the weak ones like the species that maybe grew an eye on their knee equivalent, and since that wasn't conducive to survival, died out? These failed species should exist before getting it right. Where are the species that had gills and a quarter of a lung before amphibians, with full lungs, came into existence? Well, the fossil record can't tell us that either. What does the fossil record tell us then? Evolution doesn't explain everything. There are massive holes in the debate because the fossil record has disproven Darwin without leading to a better explanation. Now the religious people are saying, "Yay! Genesis is right." Not so fast. To be fair, we have to add the same microscope we used on Darwinism to Creationism. Well... as people point out, in Genesis, plants came before the sun. But plants need the sun to survive because of photosynthesis, why would God do something that illogical and stupid? Religious defenders will say that Genesis was written by man and humans are like ants compared to God so we didn't explain it right. Let me help you say it correctly. Right now the evidence points to someone saying let there be complex organisms, and eyes, and land-dwelling animals, poof … poof …poof . This goes against all scientific understanding so I have no idea how this could possibly have happened so I say, "God did it."

Sounds like, "How come plants grow and then they die at the same time of year?"

The Greeks said, "Well, you see….. Hades, the God of the underworld, kidnapped Persephone, daughter of the goddess of the harvest, Demeter. Demeter made a deal with Hades that he could have her daughter for half the year but he had to return her for the other half. So when Demeter's daughter is taken away, she gets sad, so it gets colder and the plants die. But when the daughter returns, she's happy again so the plants come back." I honestly do not see any difference in this story and Genesis. Both use supernatural explanations to explain something we can't explain. If you say we progressed because we only have one God, whereas the Greeks had many. Well, the Egyptians had Rey, the sun God that they worshipped monotheistically. The Greeks had Zeus as the king of their gods so there is some monotheism 5,000 years ago. This is not a completely new phenomenon. Muslims have many prophets, which are like lesser Gods like the Greek gods except for Zeus. Christians do away with lesser gods with the first commandment, but is that really a progression? No, you just ignore all the others and go for the top. So, if you lived 5,000 years ago, you just ignore Apollo, Poseidon and all those lesser Gods and worship Zeus.

NYU Professor Reynolds looks at history and concludes that religion is just a mirror of the culture of the people. Greeks were constantly at war, so the Greek gods constantly warred with each other and even intervened in human wars. We live in a fearful society. We want someone to rescue us from fears. In comes the savior, Jesus Christ, God. I have trouble arguing against him. George Carlin says, "Whether you pray to the sun, the three leaf clover, God, the rabbit's foot, or Joe Pesci, your prayers get answered at about the same 50/50 rate." It may be true we have fewer stories because fewer things are unexplained but we still resort to the same method if we don't understand. This isn't progress. This is also how I justify believing in God but not organized religion. The evidence points to someone saying, "Let there be this species." It didn't happen the way Genesis said it did. Religious people say the bible is a book of salvation history so it shouldn't be completely accurate. This is dangerous because how do I separate the inaccuracies from the accuracies?

The theologian will answer, "Come to church."

Mine is, "No, I'll come to my own conclusions."

This argument is most commonly summed up with, "Those who don't know history are condemned to repeat it." People have forgotten history and what they haven't forgotten, they refuse to learn from. It may be true that as the world progresses superficially, we have more access to knowledge. That's where the Internet and I-phone$_{TM}$ come in. Despite our ability to access information effortlessly, we still learn nothing and can't avoid having these exact same problems, theories and debates that we've been having for 5,000 years.

Objectivism

I consider myself a fundamental Objectivist. What does that mean exactly? I believe everything is either black and white or right and wrong. For every argument and situation there is always a right answer and a wrong answer. The sentence, "Well it's just my opinion," is completely meaningless to me. Yes, it is your opinion but contrary to what you believe opinions can be wrong.

Objectivists will say that their creator was Ayn Rand, who was a Russian author that fled communist Russia and came to America. I would say it started, like many other schools of thought and subject, with the ancient Greeks. Socrates, Plato and Aristotle were all Objectivists. Unfortunately for mankind, there haven't been many pure Objectivists in between Plato and Ayn Rand. I guess Descartes came close, but I wouldn't consider him one. The thing I love most about being a fundamental Objectivist is that nobody else really is. Even people who love Socrates, Plato, Aristotle and Ayn Rand's books, think I go too far in my endorsement of this philosophy, which makes me love it. Socrates said, "I would rather the whole world should be at odds with me, and oppose me, rather than I myself should be at odds with myself, and contradict myself." I couldn't agree more.

First, let's get into the black and white argument. You often hear, "Nothing is black and white, there's always a grey area."

Thinking about this for a half of a second, it doesn't even make sense. Without black and white, there can be no grey since all grey is black mixed with white. If you are missing one ingredient, you can't make the whole, therefore there must be black and white.

For those moderation theorists that say, "Well some things are black and white but not everything." I'm glad you're keeping the color analogy consistent but you are still wrong and I liken it to the *Southpark* "Flatulence in moderation theory." Real quick, Kenny died because he had a girlfriend and held in his farting for too long causing him to explode. Then everyone in *Southpark* started farting whenever they felt like it, which caused problems in the environment leading to the flatulence in moderation theory: Fart in moderation. I say if you have to fart, hold it until you get a proper context in which to do so, then fart away. When someone talks about a grey area, all they mean is they're not smart enough or simply don't know what the correct answer is so they justify it to themselves by talking about the grey area so they can move on with their lives. I would just call it what it is, "I simply don't know."

The best way to arrive at the objective truth of something is by arguing.......Hence, the Socratic Method. Socrates believed in reincarnation. Since we have lived so many lives, humans know everything. But we forgot. Through the process of asking questions and seeking to answer them we can find out any answer. Well, I'm not as smart as Socrates. I continually argue with people to try to find as many objective truths as I can but I do not have all the answers. I don't even know who is right between Plato and Aristotle. When Plato said that objective truth exists, we just can't even achieve it since man is corrupted by things like Sophists. Aristotle believed that we can achieve it, it's just hard. I've wrestled with these two views knowing that one is right and the other is wrong, but I just can't decide which side I'm on. My parents are split down the middle. My dad likes Aristotle, my mom, Socrates. So I got it from both sides growing up. Though neither of my parents are fundamental Objectivists like me.

To attack the general consensus point of view that opinions can't be right or wrong, I will use an extreme example. Keep in mind the following opinion I do *not* share. People, like Iranian president Mahmoud Ahmadinejad, have the opinion that all Jews should be killed and Israel wiped off the face of the Earth. Some people may have the opinion that Hitler was right. I believe Ahmadinejad is one of them if he could just get passed his belief that the Holocaust was a hoax and it never really happened. The last part isn't an opinion, he's stating something he believes to be fact, but the first two are opinions. Both are simply wrong. Every opinion has the same right or wrong base. It's just not as easy to ascertain which it is. If you read anything in the book that you don't agree with, please say I'm wrong. Do not say, "Well it's just my opinion." Yes, it is my opinion but is the opinion right or wrong? I may even be entitled to my opinion but it's still right or wrong.

Often times in movies and media, liberals will tell conservatives that they need to respect their freedom of speech but do not respect conservatives' freedom of speech. Nobody cared when liberals called Bush a Nazi or Stalin, but when conservatives called Obama a Nazi or Karl Marx, suddenly that was wrong. Both opinions are wrong. Bush didn't kill six million people and neither did Obama, so calling them Nazis is wrong on both accounts. In movies you hear, "We say freedom of speech and freedom of expression but what about when people exercise their rights by burning the American flag?"

Well, burning the American flag is a type of treason, and they should be treated accordingly. Just because you have freedom of speech and freedom of expression, doesn't mean someone can't tell you you're wrong and take action against it. Pretty much, if you do something wrong you need to fear the consequences because people's freedoms of speech violate others, and that's how you get an argument, which is good. People who refuse to believe that when we argue it's just my opinion or come back with, "It depends on the person," annoy the hell out of me. You're wrong, one of us is right, one of us is wrong. Now let's argue and try to find out which it is. Almost always this debate ends in a stalemate, but that's part of the process.

Seeing that I make arguing come off as this beautiful thing to seek out truth, I merely say it's the best way. It is by no means perfect. After all, some people are better at arguing and rhetoric than others. That's why people choose to become Lobbyists and lawyers. They realize they're pretty good at arguing. So how do we know if the information gathered in a debate was our finding the truth or being a victim of fancy rhetoric? The best way I've found to test it is to take what you've learned and argue with someone else. The fancy rhetoric falls apart because the points are left on their own without the backing of the good arguer, and thus fall without its needed base. An objective truth does not need a base, they can stand on their own and anyone can argue the point. Of course, you run into the problem of you being a better arguer than the person you're arguing with and it's a vicious cycle. In order to get closer to the truth, however, you need to go through the cycle. Can you achieve it? That depends on if you believe Aristotle or Plato.

One of my former friend's father is a lawyer. I was extremely close with his family and loved arguing with his father because he and his siblings were afraid of him. So when they saw me hold my own against him, it emboldened them. I practically lived at their house for the better part of four years. There were many arguments that I lost and left thinking I was wrong because he convinced me. But, when I would go out and argue his points with other people, I got creamed in the argument because he didn't really prove anything. He just pretended to and spun in a way to make me think he was right when in reality he wasn't. The difference between a parrot and a human is that a human understands why he's saying what he's saying and the meaning of it. A parrot only can say the words but not the meaning. When I used his arguments, a lot of times I was just a parrot. I never would have known this if I didn't argue with other people.

Have I ever been proven wrong and it held up? Of course. I tell people I'm always right so that they will be encouraged to argue with me, and it works extremely well. But if you're going to proceed down this path, you need to have the responsibility of admitting you're wrong if proved wrong. I go into every argument hoping to find a worthy opponent to prove me wrong, but they need to earn it. This is similar to my Spartan ancestors who went into battle hoping to find a worthy opponent good enough to kill them. The Spartans didn't lose too many wars with this mentality.

It seems that other great warriors in history shared this mentality. The Samurai and Vikings also wished to die in every battle they went into. They didn't lose often as well. It's paradoxical, but it is true. Fight hoping to live, you will die. The Samurai viewed bringing a shield into battle as a sign of weakness because their opponents were hoping to live and you should never bring a tool whose sole purpose is defense in order

to try to maintain life. Likewise, I go into every argument hoping to lose
I don't lose often and it has nothing to do with fancy rhetoric. It's that
my views have been constantly tested through many arguments with
others and with myself in my lifelong pursuit to find as many objective
truths as possible.

I will give an example of when I was wrong. I often argued that
there was no logical reason not to hit women. I didn't hit women
because I was raised not to, and my father beat this message into me,
so I went through my life believing that it wasn't okay to hit women.
People often point to the argument, "Men are naturally stronger than
women, so you shouldn't hit women."

My rebuttal, "Women are naturally tougher than men, so they can
take a hit better. Therefore, it's even." Silly me, I don't think men are
superior to women nor vice versa. It's equal. Some things men are better
at it but it's equaled by the things women are better at. Nobody can
really get passed these points. Once you get rid of the common stance
and show it to be false, it is something you just shouldn't do. Even Chris
Rock who, like me, would never hit a woman, admitted there's often a
reason to. On my 19th birthday, I had this debate with one of my friends
at NYU. It went like all the others before until he said, "Yea…. but it
is more detrimental for a woman to leave a mark on her body than it is
for a male, so you do more harm than just pain."

I thought hard about this argument and immediately things rushed
into my head. For instance, women have thinner skin than men,
therefore it is easier to bruise or leave a mark. I know men who brag
about the scars they have, and if I had big scars, I would too. Women
just cannot do that. A woman's appearance is infinitely more important
than a man's and that's true for any culture. Therefore, because of the
way society is set up you shouldn't hit women because you cause more
harm than just the pain of the fight, which is really the only harm the
man faces. He effectively proved me wrong and I have argued this point
with others, and nobody has proven this point wrong to date. Oddly,
years later we talked about this point and he couldn't reformulate his
brilliant argument. That's okay. It doesn't change the fact that he was
right. When Bill Maher did *Religious* he didn't have this responsibility
because someone explained how Christianity is monotheistic by saying,
"Think of water, it can be steam, ice or water depending if it's liquid,

solid or gas, but it's still the same thing." He admitted this was a legit point but the very next scene he said, "Yea, but if you think about it for half a second you realize it's ridiculous. What? God is this little gas floating in the air, that's ridiculous." Sorry Bill, he got you, you just couldn't admit it.

For those of you who still believe that there is no objective reality, like the Sophists did, I'll frame the argument this way:

> You just told me, there is no objective truth. If there was no objective truth, then that sentence is wrong because the sentence, in and of itself, is an objective truth. So you just contradicted yourself.

This argument is blatantly stolen from my theology teacher. He said it in class when I was an atheist. Since his argument didn't mutually distinguish God from Objective truth, I had to save myself by coming up with the brilliant rendition of, "The only objective truth is that there is no objective truth." I went with that for a while, until I realized that I'm saying, "There is no objective truth" is an objective truth and the fact that it's the only one is another objective truth. I then tried, "There are no objective truths outside of this sentence." That fit my profile, but even I believed I was stretching it. Then I read Ayn Rand and realized that objective truths exist, it's subjectivism that doesn't.

If you said: "Who are you to say what are the truths and what aren't"?

My answer is you completely missed the entire point of this chapter and I have never claimed to be the one that determines it.

Objective truths exist outside of man. It's like the invisible hand that I love so much in economics. People tell me "Why don't we just print enough money to pay off the national debt?"

I respond: "That would cause massive inflation."

Their rebuttal: "No, just have the government not tell anyone they printed all the money so that way people don't raise their prices."

This causes me to marvel in how clueless people are about economics. I don't know, maybe Bill O'Reilly thinks this to be a fair point. Bottom line is...... it doesn't matter if you don't tell anyone. The invisible hand will make it happen. How it works is extremely complex and not something I fully understand I just know it does. If you want a historical basis, Germany printed a lot of money to pay reparations after World War I. It caused hyperinflation to the point that restaurants stopped printing menus and just wrote the prices on a maker board because it changed every hour. This is horrifying to Greeks like me who when we all get together can have three hour dinners, the price would have raised three times. I can't imagine a society like this and can't explain to you how it worked, I just know it happened.

Objective truth works in the same way as the invisible hand. No matter how many people you convince it doesn't exist, it has absolutely no effect on its power. If you convince the world you are a certain way, you never really convince yourself and your real self will break out. Everyone believed the earth was flat before Columbus ......It didn't change the fact they were all wrong. Even Socrates, Aristotle and Plato believed the Earth to be the center of the universe. ...It didn't change the fact they were wrong. It is ego-centric to disbelieve the world only exists through human eyes. The world truths existed long before we got here, and it will continue when we're gone. Nobody determines what objective truths are, they just try to figure them out.

Racism and the People Who Cry It

As I remark in my "Stereotypes and Generalities" chapter, everyone is a little racist. I distinguish racism from stereotypes and generalities because racism adds a negative connotation that goes beyond stereotypes and generalities. The point is that America is the least racist country on Earth. That doesn't mean it's perfect, a few people have done everything in their power to keep the racial divide in America, and they do a pretty good job. After all, if people knew the truth, that people weren't as racist as those people would like us to believe, they would have significantly less money, and that just won't cut it for them. Before I attack people who cry racism almost every day of their lives, I'll explore other countries.

Now, I have not been to every country, I've been to 23 of them and that's including the United States. I will tell you stories from my travels and you tell me if your United States experience compares. In 2004, near Piazza Michelangelo in Florence, Italy, an American couple was sitting on a lawn that they may or may not have known was not public property. For those of you that have never been to Piazza Michelangelo, it is an elevated part of the city that offers a stunning view of Florence from above and has a copy of the statue of David along with some mermaids around it. I believe this to be the most scenic part of Florence and would encourage you to visit. While the couple was sitting admiring the view, the man who owned the property came out and began screaming at the couple. They were Americans and didn't understand Italian so they yelled back in English. Since most Italians speak English, I tend to believe that the property owner just was ignoring them because he was defending his property. Everyone has a right to defend their property and he is not at fault for doing so. The property owner took out a knife and stabbed the American tourist killing him. He was arrested and when he went to court his defense to the judge was, "Your honor, I thought he was Albanian."

The judge looked at the pictures, the American tourist had dark features and concluded he did look Albanian and reduced the man's sentence presumably because the man merely thought he was killing an Albanian. In case you haven't been able to figure this out, Italians don't like Albanians. This is because Albanians illegally enter nearby countries, like Italy, and cause crime and con their way into various government programs pretending to be locals when they are not. Unlike the illegal immigrants in from Mexico and Latin America, Albanians are not interested in finding jobs, they merely create trouble there. Now, for as long as I've been living in America, I've never heard someone use this defense, let alone have it work to reduce a sentence. That is racism. Dave Chappelle says that he is a connoisseur of racism from his travels and says that the south is the epitome. Dave, please pay more attention. When you travel to other countries as Chappelle has, because that's real racism that cannot be found in the south who only use n-word but are still hospitable to Black people. Italians are not hospitable if they find out someone is Albanian.

Another example is less clear on if it's racism. My own bias leads me to believe it is but you can be the judge. At the Fontagne di Trevi in Rome, a gypsy woman was holding what presumed to be a baby near the fountain. For those of you who don't know, the Fontagne di Trevi is a huge ornate fountain in Rome with various statues of horses, people and the like. There are a lot of fountains in Rome, this is by far the coolest and most famous. As she neared the fountain, her arms started getting nearer to it. There were little kids not too far behind her. It seemed to be her plan was to pretend to lose her grip on the baby prompting people around her to lean over to help meanwhile the little kids pickpocket them. For those of you who don't know, Gypsies are amazingly good pickpocketers. They practice by taking a necklace of bells off a walking person without ringing the bells. Their logic, and I agree, is if you can do that, you can take something out of a person's pocket without them knowing. An Italian was on the other side of the fountain and saw the gypsy, he immediately went into a dead sprint, jump kicked a little kid in stride and punted the baby out of the woman's arms into the fountain. The Gypsies scurried away, meanwhile the tourists scolded him. He merely pointed out that the doll that the Gypsy was passing off as a baby was floating and babies don't float. Now, he claimed he was 100% positive that it wasn't a real baby. I don't believe this because there is no way he could have been able to tell that that wasn't a baby from the other side of the fountain. What I think is that he really didn't care if it was a baby or not. They're Gypsies and I don't think he really would mind punting a gypsy into a fountain. He certainly had no trepidation to jump kick the little kid. That act was completely unnecessary but I'd think he'd respond, "They're Gypsies, it's okay." I've known some people who claim to be racist by American standards, but I've never seen them jump kick little Black or Hispanic kids like this guy did.

If you think I'm lying, simply ask a European the question, "What groups of people do you hate?' and they will answer honestly. An American would say, "I'm not racist at all" and get mad at you for even suggesting it...not a European.

A similar conversation to this came up when I was in Greece with my cousins. I love Greek music and I told them this. At that time, I loved Lefteris Pentazhs, who is a Greek singer that wrote a song that was a major hit with the Greek-American community called "Φιλακια" (pronounced fee-la-kia) or kisses. It was translated by a Greek American into English, but it wasn't very popular in any community. During the chorus, they actually made the noise for kisses, so it's universally known what they're doing. Inevitably when I told my cousins I like Greek music, they asked me which singers or bands. I started rattling off the ones I like and when I got to Pentazhs, they immediately got stern faced. They were astounded that I could like him and said so. After a while, they tried to give me a chance to save myself and said, "Well at least you don't like the song, Φιλακια right?"

I responded that was one of my favorite songs and they let me have it. Finally, I found out why. Pentazhs stole that song from a Turkish singer, translated it into Greek and sang it. Because of this, most Greeks hated him and boycotted his CD's. His CD may have been popular in America but not in Greece. That is how deep their hatred for the Turks runs. They had only gotten their independence in 1825, so it's about as recent as slavery here. Although this is somewhat equaled by the lead singer of the Fugees when she said, "I'd rather see a Black boy starve than a White person buy my CD." I believe the Greek boycott of a fellow Greek just because he took one song from a Turk to be a little more vitriolic. My cousin then unscrupulously told me, "Listen, here is the order of people Greeks hate 1) Turks 2) Albanians 3) Jews 4) French 5) Americans. I was so happy that the French were ranked higher than us. Now the problem with me following suit with the first one the way they want me to is that all but one Turkish person I've met has been a really nice person who was easy to get along with. My track record isn't that good with almost all other nationalities. Maybe only Turkish-Americans are nice, but even when I went to Turkey they weren't rude. Even when I accidentally spoke Greek to them out of habit since I was coming from Greece, the person politely told me it would be safer to not speak Greek in Turkey. They tried to get me to buy things, but that's not mean spirited. They're poor and trying to provide for their family. I have no qualms about that even if they're trying to rip me off. People try to rip me off in New York every day, I'm used to this.

Another example of Greeks' racism for the Turks is when I was in London with my family. It was kind of late and we were eating at a Turkish restaurant. There weren't many restaurants open at the time, and Greek tourists came up saying that they were really hungry and were happy to see a restaurant. That is until they realized it was Turkish. Since my mom is like most Greeks and can't help herself to speak Greek to people she hears speaking Greek, she greeted them in Greek. They turned to my mom appalled and asked the first two questions that Greeks always start with when meeting someone they think is Greek. 1) Are you Greek? 2) What part of Greece are you from? They judge you accordingly by the second question. After they got through that, she became more appalled and asked my mom if she was aware of what kind of restaurant she was eating at. She replied, "Yea, it's Turkish."

Now my mom knows the dynamics of Greece and the rivalry but she can't help but being brutally honest, a trait I have taken from her.

The woman immediately yelled at us for eating at a Turkish restaurant and calling us disgraces to Greeks. My mom's response, "We were hungry."

The woman and the man she was with, presumably her husband, stormed off. We knew they were hungry too but they would rather go hungry until they found another place to eat than eat at a Turkish restaurant and we were disgraces to Greeks for eating there. Welcome to real racism.

At least Greece and Turkey will let each other enter the country (Only for a maximum three days). Dubai won't even do that. In Dubai, if you have an Israeli passport you are not allowed in the country. If you're not from Israel but are Jewish, they interrogate you as to why you want to enter Dubai and make it very uncomfortable to do so. I really have no problem with this policy, it's their country. If they don't want the money from Jewish and Israeli tourists, that's their prerogative, but it is clearly racist and not equaled in America.

Now, Hispanics have a very strange form of racism, especially Dominicans and Puerto Ricans. Ask a Dominican what they think of a Puerto Rican or vice versa and see what kind of response you get. Sometimes they'll deny it, but then when you call them the other, they get really mad, even if the questions come back to back. They don't mind this contradiction apparently. As a teaser to how their racism is, I'll tell you a story to put this in perspective. My roommate's friend is Puerto Rican. They were talking about racial slurs and he said, "Yea, I don't care about that stuff, you can call me a 'spic' I don't care. It doesn't bother me."

My roommate tested it, and he wasn't offended. I then said, "What if I called you Dominican?"

He responded, "Oh hell no, mmm hmmm mmm hmm, those are fighting words nigger, don't be saying that shit."

Keep in mind I didn't call him Dominican, I merely asked him what he would say if, hypothetically speaking, I would. He had an angry response. Since I know this rivalry very well, I responded, "Then how come you have so many Dominican friends?" As I just chronicled, to a European this question would be ridiculous and they probably would question your sanity, they just told you they hated them, why would they be friends with them?

His response was, "Oh to their face I be all nice and say what's up, how are you, but when they turn around, I be talking, I be talking."

I want to point out this was the first time I ever met this guy and I had no idea who his friends were except my Irish roommate that makes me look brown. How did I know he had Dominican friends you ask? The more vehemently a Dominican or a Puerto Rican reacts to the other, the closer they are to one of the opposite. I was at a party with one of my closest friends who is Dominican by descent. The party consisted of her cousins and a couple other non-Hispanics. The DJ played a song whose chorus is, "Puerto Rico ooooo" . She walked up to the DJ and yelled at him for playing a Puerto Rican song at a Dominican party. Now, I know this girl. She is married to a Puerto Rican, that's as close as it gets. Therefore, she will talk the loudest against them. That is why she was the only person there that felt the need to yell at the DJ for playing the song when there were so many other Dominicans present. It works the other way too. I went out with a Venezuelan co-worker and she introduced me to her Puerto Rican friend. I said to her, "What do you think of Dominicans?"

She said, "See…. I don't understand the whole rivalry they have, I have no problem with them at all. I mean we're such similar cultures, so we really shouldn't be fighting each other so much."

Given what I've learned, I responded, "Then how come you don't have any Dominican friends?"

Again, I just met her; I have no idea who her friends are except my Venezuelan Co-worker. She responded, "Well, it's not because I'm racist toward them it just happens to be that way."

The more vigorously they debate they hate the other, the closer they are, it's directly proportional and it's on both the Puerto Rican and Dominican side equally. This is fascinating to me because it adds an entirely different angle to racism. By the way, if you talk to other Hispanics they will say they don't like Dominicans and Puerto Ricans because they speak bad Spanish and other insults. To their credit, Dominicans and Puerto Ricans admit they have bad Spanish because they cut off letters such as "e" and "s" in order to speak quicker. This is why if you have heard someone say, "Ta Bien" they are not saying "Tambien" which means "me too," the way I mistook it at first. Really they're saying "Esta Bien or Estas bien" meaning, "It's good" or, in this context, "Okay." They just don't say e's and s's. For those who point out I included the "e" in "Bien" well it's not very pronounced in that word as it is in "Esta."

By comparison, if you look at the five groups Greek people hate, you have to get down to four for people they actually will associate with. Dominicans and Puerto Ricans are that way with number one.

Now that we got into real racism and the two forms of racism by race, we will talk about the people who cry racism and the hidden forms. Liberals cry racism all the time and they are the most racist people in America. Take affirmative action. Besides the obvious fact of it being reverse racism in that White people are denied a job because of the color of their skin just to fulfill some quota that the government imposes, it's racist to Blacks too. Think about what affirmative action is actually saying, "Blacks can't succeed without White people's help."

White liberals made these laws and believe it to be the only way minorities will enter the work force. Conservatives say, "Bullshit, Blacks don't need White people's help to succeed, they can do it on their own."

Since most businesses are run by conservatives, I would say they know what they're talking about. Employers do see in color, but it's green not black and white. They will hire anybody and everybody that will make their bottom line, which is their profit, higher. That's all they really care about. Why do you think restaurant owners and businesses hire illegal immigrants? They work harder and for less pay than anyone else. If you get to pay your workers less, profits are higher. This isn't even a new strategy. When the Irish came here during the potato famine, employers put up signs, "No Irish need apply." Seems kind of similar to, "White only" don't you think? So the Irish did all the shit jobs nobody wanted, and worked their way up from there to even having an Irish president in John F. Kennedy. Yes, African Americans got a president before the Hispanics, but they did get a head start. The Hispanics already got a Supreme Court justice, this working your way up through hard work thing seems to work.

I argued reverse racism a.k.a. affirmative action in a number of my classes. The explanation by the professors was always moronic. Given that college professors are generally stupid, I guess I shouldn't be too surprised. One professor cited a book that argued that opponents of affirmative action are wrong, that more Whites would be let in because of affirmative action. He uses the analogy of a parking lot that has handicap parking and people circling trying to find a parking spot. If there were no handicap spots, people would still be circling. Yes, they would if there are more people circling than there are handicap spots. What exactly is your point? Are you saying minorities are handicapped? Well yes, that is what affirmative action is saying so the analogy seems to work.

Are you saying that if there was no affirmative action, some Whites still wouldn't be admitted? I agree, but I've never heard someone say that without affirmative action no White person would ever be rejected when applying for a job or school. In your analogy, if there were no handicap spots, there would be fewer people circling, which is better than having more people circling. Based on your analogy, I think you're arguing my position. The only problem with it is that I think it's fair to say that if you have a condition that warrants a handicap pass, you cannot walk as well as someone who doesn't. I don't think it's fair to say if you're a minority you can't perform as well in school as a non-minority. Maybe I'm too stupid to see the brilliance of the analogy and how it completely blows opponents of affirmative action out of the water.

Even the desegregation movement was littered with inconsistencies. It seemed to be based on the assumption that Black is inferior to White. In order to prove racism, there's a common test in which they show students of early ages, in schools where Whites are the majority, a black doll and a white doll are shown and the testers ask the children which they think is better. A majority of them pick the white one. Interestingly though, when you do this test in schools where Blacks are the majority, you get a higher percentage of students that pick the white doll. The second part of the study is conveniently left out when people bring this one up, I wonder why?

It is truer that Blacks are racist toward Whites than vice versa. You just only hear about the Whites being racist toward Blacks. Blacks are allowed to form Black-only clubs, fraternities, sororities and other groups on public campuses, Whites can't do the same thing. Employers are forced to hire a certain number of Black people not a certain number of Whites. Despite this blatant unfairness, White people are employed more than Blacks and do better as a whole. This is because regardless of what laws you put into place, hard work will always win. This is why the gap between White success and Hispanic success is blurred. Hispanics work harder than Whites, so they are gaining on us and probably will surpass us. I say good, hard work should pay off.

The liberal media couldn't wait to chronicle all the abuses Black students got when they went to White schools but they ignored the Blacks who harassed the White people bused to Black schools. I know of a woman who talks about how she would try to walk down the hall but students would pick her up over her shoulder and carry her to other side stopping her from going to class. She still managed to become valedictorian, and at graduation during her speech, she was repeatedly interrupted by boos and people yelling out, "I ain't going to have no cracker be my valedictorian."

Why is it okay for Blacks to treat Whites this way but not vice versa? Racist media, racist laws… Racism is not the answer to racism. Everyone is created equal. The way things are given to Black people it seems the common Black mother saying to her child, "Nobody will ever give you anything," is a lie.

Personally, I believe that affirmative action was put into place to keep Black people down. After all, it's human nature not to fight for something or appreciate something when it's given to you. People need to be motivated, I don't know if I would have worked so hard to get into NYU and succeed if I knew that I didn't have to score as high as everybody else. Despite all these programs, Blacks always score last among Whites and Hispanics across the board in academic prowess and most Hispanics don't have the luxury of being brought up knowing English from their parents. This natural advantage doesn't seem to help them against Hispanics though.

Some argue that since Whites are normally wealthier, they have access to classes like Princeton Review for help on nationalized tests. I would say this promotes my point because they assume if you're Black, you're poor and if you're White, you're rich, which is consistent with my stereotypes but is also racist. Do I have a better way? Of course I do. These college applications ask for household incomes anyway so why not just have one more thing to fill out that says how much you pay in property taxes. See….. property taxes are lower in poor neighborhoods than rich. That way, you don't unfairly discriminate against poor White kids and don't unfairly help rich Black kids.

Another example comes from Thomas Weeds' *The Politically Incorrect Guide to American History*. Here is another case of liberals trying to help in the form of Andrew Johnson. In 1965, he vowed to help the unemployed by taking them out of their slums into rural conservation camps to train them in new skills. While there, the recruits were charged with a variety of crimes such as burglary, window smashing, and sodomy. The one third who managed to graduate showed no difference between people who were invited to go but didn't show up. The cost of this program would be equivalent to paying for all 100,000 or so to go to Harvard. 12% of people got a job in which they were trained for, 44% got a job at all and the average rate of pay was $ 5.09 an hour for a program that spent $ 21,333 per client. By all standards, this is a failure. In the late 1990's Bill Clinton increased funding to Job Corps to "End welfare as we know it." It didn't succeed then either. When you don't make people work for it, they will take it for granted and not utilize it, hence the Job Corp disaster. You can't throw money at the problem. You need to remove all race-based affirmative action so that people are motivated to work hard to get to where they want to be. With the way the country has gone since the desegregation movement, it is no wonder that we have the problems we have now with Barak Obama. I chronicled this point in my chapter "President Obama and the Dramatic Shift of America in 2009."

The other thing that minorities love to do is say that police officers are racist. When I ask them to elaborate they say things like...... they get pulled over every time they drive a car, or when they walk outside, cops question them. I hate to break it to you minorities, cops harass everybody. Now my cousin is a cop and my uncle was on the force for about 20 years until he got his pension for time well served. I have the utmost respect for cops and, for the most part, they're really good people. Like all groups, however, there are bad apples and I am actually going to focus on the exceptions here. As you see in my "Generalities and Stereotypes" chapter, there's a reason for stereotyping. So if cops use racial profiling, I have no problem with that. A guy I worked with got his car back because they found Black people driving it and thought it might be stolen. They were right. This racial profiling, however, goes both ways. A White woman was driving in East Cleveland, which is an extremely dangerous city on par with Compton, CA. (Compton is a city in southern Los Angeles County, California) Police officers surrounded the car and forced her out as they checked the car for drugs. They theorized that if a White woman was in East Cleveland, she had to be a drug lord. Unfortunately for the cops, she wasn't. She was actually involved in community service to help poor children. Police officers have a lot of experience to go into their schemas, when they're wrong, they generally admit it and let the person go. This is nothing to get really mad about.

Now I like police officers. This is in spite of the fact that I have been pulled over for no reason, given bogus tickets, had three sobriety test back to back to back because a police officer refused to believe that I would take a nap in my car at two in the morning and not be drunk, and here's the kicker, like I said before, I've been molested by a law enforcement agent (secret service). What I say to minorities is if you can beat this, then maybe you can talk but don't give me this shit about how you got pulled over or asked to turn the music down when you had a party that went on till 4 AM in a suburban neighborhood in Long Island. Cops harass people just the same of all races, it's part of their job description, but when shit hits the fan, you and me alike want them around to help.

Now it is time for the most controversial part of my racism chapter. I didn't really get into racial slurs in this chapter and I would be remiss if I were not to comment on them. There are a variety of ethnic slurs but I will focus on some of the most common ones. Some people ask me for an ethnic slur for Greeks. I do not know of any off hand except for "Wog." It is said to be Australian and British in origin. I've been to England but never Australia. Though I've met Australians, I was never called a Wog by either. According to Wikipedia, wog, "Usually refers to any person of South Asian, Mediterranean, Southern European, and Middle Eastern descent. Often used for Italians, Greeks, and Arabs."

I guess I'll be offended because you're grouping me with Arabs and that is a problem. The beauty is that since I'm White, you can use any racial slur or insult you want. Something Whites aren't allowed to do with minorities, which is unjust, unfair, and just downright illogical. Let me tell you how ethnic slurs would work in an objective world.

We will start with an ethnic slur more popular in America for White people. That is "cracker.". Now, I do not get offended by "cracker.". I've been called it several times by Blacks (I don't say African-American because that would leave out Jamaicans, Hatians, and even some Hispanics. After all, technically David Ortiz is Dominican but if you look at him, you may be confused where he belongs.) Hispanics and I chuckle every time. I chuckle for a variety of reasons 1) the view I'm about to get into how objectively, "cracker" is more offensive than "Nigger/Nigga" and 2) the origin of the racial slur. "Cracker" originated because slaves would call their owners that because they crack whips against their back. The slave owners were the crackers, literally the ones who did the cracking (of the whip). So, if you call me a "cracker" are you saying that I'm your master? Sorry, I believe all men are created equal, I am not your master. I do not want to house and feed you in exchange for labor. God gave me hands and feet. I have never cracked a whip against someone's back in my life, so I couldn't really be a "cracker" could I? So clearly I am not your master as I've never met you and you do not serve me. Are you saying that I should crack a whip across you back? I mean I wouldn't want you to be wrong and look foolish would I? If you call me "cracker" and I whip you with a whip, then I'm merely proving your point. Unfortunately though, I really don't want to whip you. First of all, I don't have a whip and secondly, even if I did, you really haven't done anything to warrant me whipping you yet. Sorry buddy, you're going to have to just be wrong on this case.

All joking aside, "cracker" is objectively more racist and worse than the Black or African-American equivalent. White people do not call each other "cracker" unless they're mocking minorities who speak Ebonics. At no time is the term used other than as an ethnic slur. Since nobody calls White people "cracker" unless they mean to insult them or be confrontational with them, "cracker" should be the most offensive ethnic slur. It isn't alone at the top, but it should be up there since that can be its only meaning. There are no derivations and no other way it's used. I've repeated myself but I really don't see anything more I can say on the subject.

The term "spic" originated because Hispanics say, "I don't spic

English" with their accents. A lot less cool than the derivation of "cracker" but hey, I didn't make it up. It is sometimes spelled "spik." When dealing with ethnic slurs, I don't think spelling should be your main concern. I've hung out with a number of Hispanics and they don't call each other "spics" either. They do call each other "nigga" which is kind of interesting since that's supposed to be a Black thing but they don't greet each other by "spic." I guess if you think of the origin, how do you make fun of someone for having an accent when you do as well? When people call someone a "spic," like "cracker," it is exclusively used to insult. Also like "cracker," it is used in a mocking form when imitating other people. All mocking aside, "spic" is just as bad as "cracker" in my analysis.

There is no logical reason why "nigger" or "nigga" should be that bad. Its derivation, like "Spic" is pretty boring. The Spanish and Portuguese "Negro" which is what slave owners used to call them combined with the Latin "niger" came out "nigger" then Ebonics formed "nigga."

The reason why it should not be that offensive is because African-Americans and Hispanics use this term all the time to greet each other and even White people whom they like. I've had Hispanics refer to me as "my nigga." When you ask them why they would use the term "nigger" when it's offensive, they say, "I'm not saying "nigger" I'm saying "nigga." Well I have trouble distinguishing the sounds of each because sometimes it definitely sounds like they have an "er" at the end. Even if they don't, if I clearly said, "nigga" to a Black or Hispanic I didn't know, would they be okay with it? I wouldn't try it if I were you. That's why this argument is completely false. "nigger" and "nigga" are interchangeable. Therefore, from here on in, I'm using "n-word" to describe both the "er" and "a" version. Again, I'm using "n-word" because Whites who don't use that word in a quote, are ostracized.

If you refer to yourself or others as a n-word, you can't be offended if someone calls you that. Think about when you introduce yourself, you're telling the person what you want them to call you. If they see others use different names and you respond, then anybody can use that term. The rules should not change based on who is saying them. Does it? Of course, but in an objective context devoid of emotion, if you call yourself and others it, then you should be prepared to be called one too. Chris Rock in his stand up "Bigger and Blacker" gives a very good description on the difference between Black people and n-words. Listen to it as I can't do better. I will add one thing to it. A n-word will call himself and others a n-word, a Black person will not. If you call someone a n-word and you've never heard them use that term, you are not justified, but the second they call others and themselves it, it's fair game. I don't know how Chris Rock refers to his friends. From what I could tell, he uses "n-word" only to describe the types of Black people he doesn't like. Given that, if you call him that, you are indicating you don't like him. I love Chris Rock so I would never call him that.

In Spike Lee's *Do the Right Thing* the argument is made that Sal, a pizza owner in Bedford Stuyvesant, Brooklyn, has a son that is openly racist. A Black pizza delivery boy pulls him aside and talks about how he loves Magic Johnson and other Black athletes. After he points this out, he tells him "They're all niggers." That's not true. I have never heard Magic Johnson refer to himself or others as a n-word, therefore, he is Black. As for the pizza deliverer since he didn't use the term as derogatory but for all Black people, he is an n-word. As Samuel L Jackson said in *Coach Carter*, "If you want people to stop calling you 'nigger' stop calling each other it."

Other racial slurs follow the same rules. I have a close lesbian friend. I have never heard her, her girlfriend or any of her lesbian friends use the term "dyke," Therefore, I would never call them that. I went to visit one of my homosexual friends when he lived in India. He was living with a lesbian, who by all accounts was a nice girl. She used the term "dyke" in every other sentence. One night, the three of us went out for coffee. My friend, who despite most of my friends being female is the biggest feminist of all my friends, said in response to her constant use of the word "dyke," "I feel like that's offensive."

I inserted, "Yea me too."

She said to me, "If you said it, it would be"

No, either it is offensive or it's not. If you call yourself and other's "dyke" I can too. She's a "dyke," Every other lesbian I've met is not. Hopefully you can figure out that she's the only lesbian I met that calls herself that.

When I see how free minorities are to use "cracker" and we can't respond in turn, I mark it down as just one more illogical thing about the world. No rational argument can be put forth why "n-word" is more offensive than "cracker." The term doesn't even mean you're inferior to me, it just means "Black" in a mixture of two languages. It isn't reminiscent of slavery times because "Negro" was used more often back then. Even if it was, slavery has been over for over 200 years. It's completely irrational to suggest that's what I'm thinking. And if you will go to that point, "cracker" is reminiscent of slavery so if your argument is that anything is offensive that references slavery, then that would mean when Blacks call us "cracker" it is offensive to Black people. So, they're offending themselves? Luckily when Whites get called "cracker" they don't think of the context. If they did, there would be a lot more hate crimes.

Oddly enough, it's only a hate crime if a White person attacks a minority, minorities can attack Whites and it's just assault or battery, we get a whole new charge added to it. In this millennium, the most discriminated race in America is the White Catholic male, and guess which group does extremely well in society?..........the White Catholic male. The reason is not bias or favoritism. It's because White Catholic males continue to work hard no matter how much laws and society packs against them because they know that hard work always beats government and societal favoritism in the long run. White Catholic males understand that nothing will be handed to them. Everyone gets free reign to attack them, but they will rise above it.

Similarly, Jews are the most discriminated race on the planet. Yet everywhere they go, they succeed because they stick together and help each other out. They're also smart, hard working and extremely disciplined. That's how they rise above world racism and succeed no matter what country they're in or how visceral the hatred. I wish Greek people were more like the Jews. We fight amongst each other unless there's an outside force invading, and then we unite, get rid of them and go back to fighting each other. This has been true for 5,000 years. That's why today in Astoria, New York, the city with the highest concentration of Greek people, some of the Greek diner owners will call the health board on nearby diners hoping that they find something to shut them down. Jews do not do this.

It's because of all this, why I have no sympathy for Black people and am appalled with "White Man Burden." It's not our fault they're not succeeding, it's theirs.

ABORTION

Now we come to my biggest liberal view, I am pro-abortion. All the liberals just got mad at me for calling it that instead of "pro-choice" . I don't believe in euphemisms. I call it what it is. I am not ashamed. The other thing I love is liberals get mad at me for this view because they claim I argue for abortion in a conservative way. Well, what did you expect? I would only pick one issue to be a moron on?

With abortion, future criminals are killed and in the end the loss of the one life could save a number of others and save the state money from incarcerating them or supporting them. As I said before, 80% of the people that are in juvenile hall are adopted. An estimated 90% of homeless people were also adopted. So if a program comes along that will attack 80% of the juvenile delinquents and 90% of the homeless, I like it. Adoption simply doesn't work because it is a fate worse than death for a child to know that they were not wanted by their biological parents. Since kids are rude to their biological parents, they definitely don't feel like they should take orders from non-biological ones and often times tell them this with comebacks like, "You're not my real mother."

Steven Levitt & Stephen Dubner do a great job in describing this in *Freakonomics*. If you ask me, they did a little too good of a job of this. I had been arguing this point for years, until I argued with someone who read the book who came back with, "Oh you just read that in *Freakonomics*.".

I had never heard of the book before. I boycotted it for two years because I was upset that someone came up with the same idea I did and actually published it so I can't get credit for being the originator now. Eventually, I did read it because I got over myself and my ego and decided that this person was smart enough to come up with something I had seen nobody else come up with. So maybe they had some other cool insights. I enjoyed the book then e-mailed Professor Levitt and apologized for boycotting his book. He just responded, "Better late than never."

It had to be a weird e-mail. If I had received a similar e-mail, I don't know how I would have reacted. I think I would just respond the same way Professor Levitt did. Anyway, his book actually helped me. While in Kentucky, I decided to look up the crime rate from 1990 – 1995 by state. My argument was that the states that decreased in crime would have high abortion rates. I chose 1990-1995 because *Roe v. Wade* was 1978. The first kids to be adopted would be between 12-17, which is the age most juvenile crimes take place. My first obstacle was that every state with the exception of West Virginia saw a decrease in crime between those years. I added another column to do sheer number decrease. There are 10 states with above average abortion rates and they ranked sporadically in sheer number decrease. New York saw the biggest decrease, but I attribute that to Giuliani's work not so much abortion. I was discouraged by these results but I did keep them. After I read *Freaonomics,* Levitt did similar studies and said it worked. I don't remember which years he picked, but he did say you could pick any time period and find similar results so long as 1978 babies would reach an age where they were capable of crimes. His variation of it was not by sheer number decease but percentage decrease. I went back to my data and put anther column calculating the percentage decrease. Of the ten states that have above abortion rates, five of them were ranked #s 1-5 in the country. Obviously if all ten were 1-10, it would be perfect, but in the real world there are other factors that contribute. The world doesn't happen in a vacuum devoid of all controlled variables except the one you're testing. The fact that you had to go to sixth in the country in percentage decrease to find one of the 40 states with average or below average abortion rates is about as good as it gets.

For those liberals that still try to argue about how it's a woman's body she should have a choice what she wants to do. Or, who are you as a man to tell a woman what to do with her body? These are weak arguments. One, the man had something to do with creating the baby too so he should get some say. More importantly, it isn't really part of her body. It's just growing inside it. Some babies don't even have the same blood type as their mother, and despite your arguments to the contrary, it is alive and it is human. Just because you can't exist outside the womb, doesn't make it non-human. Doctors have performed miracles in incubators with pre-mature babies and science keeps finding out just how early heart beats and fingernails develop. The more information we get, the more this argument falls apart. Even my hero Ayn Rand fell short when trying to justify abortion. Her argument was that fetuses have the potential to become humans and potential doesn't mean actuality. In her day, they didn't understand the development of a fetus the way we do now.

For you pro-lifers who argue that it psychologically affects the mother, well so does having an unwanted child or giving it up for adoption. No matter what option she takes, she's going to be emotionally affected. After all, women have an innate attraction to their babies. What about post-partum depression? It's so common, there's a name for it.

The other bullshit pro-life argument is when they chronicle how disgusting the abortion surgery is. Well I got news for you, surgery is disgusting. I've seen videos of my father's eye surgeries, which compared to most surgeries is pretty tame, but even that bothered me. I saw him make a cut on the eye to lift up the cornea so he could laser inside. My eyes began to water just from looking at it. Just the thought of sticking things into your eye is a little weird to me and I do it every day to put contacts in. Once you get into open-heart surgery and you get all the blood and seeing the organs, that's not something I want to have lunch too, and I actually have a pretty strong stomach.

Let's just pretend that abortion surgery is the only disgusting looking surgery. Birth is extremely disgusting. It is so disgusting, in fact, that my health class showed us a live birth as a form of contraception. They wanted us to be so grossed out by a birth that we would not have sex in fear of that happening. My friend brought her 16-year-old niece into her room as she was giving birth for the same purpose. It had the desired effect as the teenager walked in and said, "I'm not having kids for a very very long time."

As I look at the pro-life debates, I can't see any logic in them. If put to my previous criteria, if something is a good idea, do you help more people than you hurt? Yes you do. Having an unwanted baby affects you, those closest to you, the kid who has to live knowing his biological parents didn't want him, and you increase the likelihood of having another violent criminal that will cause physical harm to other people. If you have an abortion, you kill the baby, hurt yourself but help your family and those closest to you as well as the people that the kid most likely would have physically harmed. That sounds like a fair trade to me.

GLOBAL WARMING

This is another subject that Bill O'Reilly conveniently only gives one side of the story. Whenever he gets someone on that tells him global warming is a myth, he tells them to buy a thermometer. Have there been record high temperatures somewhere in the world? Yes. Have there been record cold temperatures in the last couple years somewhere in the world? Yes. What exactly is this thermometer that I bought telling me then? Some places it's record cold. In others, record hot. What does that mean?

Well if you watch the movie, *The Day After Tomorrow* both statistics prove global warming. I'm shocked people can say this with a straight face. In the 70s, experts predicted the temperature would rise 3.3 degrees by the year 2000. It rose 1.1 degree. These experts then bragged about how good they were because they were proven right. My response is that you were 300% off. In what other situation can you be 300% off and then demand praise? If you got an estimate on repairs for your car and were told it would cost you $ 1,000.00 then they repaired it and charged you $ 3,000.00 would you be like, "Wow, the mechanic gave me a really good estimate"?

Something tells me you'd be extremely upset with the mechanic and would probably never go there again. If you were given a project and you told your boss you'd have it done in two days. Then you come back six days later and then bragged to your boss that you kept your word, you said two days and it took you six. Your boss would probably think you're delusional and the conversation wouldn't go in your favor. Weathermen can't even predict the weather tomorrow with great accuracy, let alone in 30 years. My point is, admit it. You were 300% off, which is not something to write home about.

When I was younger, I read animal books because I loved animals. I remember in fifth grade reading about my favorite animal, the Siberian tiger. I cried when I read that all Siberian tigers would be extinct by the year 2000. It is now 2009 and the Siberian tiger is not extinct. I have not read anything about their recovery. Some will say it's because they're protected but they've been protected for a while. Why is it that whenever they make a prediction and they're wrong, they claim how good they are at predicting? In fact, can someone find one example where a long term weather prediction was made and they were right?

I would also love to have so many people believe an argument like global warming. Take my abortion argument. I say that states with the higher percentage of abortions will witness a larger decrease in crime. Then I say, "Whether or not the crime rate goes up or down it proves my theory and a tenth of a percentage is extremely significant. The only way to prove me wrong is if the crime rate stays exactly the same to the tenth of a percentage." Good luck proving me wrong.

If you can't see the absurdity in the above argument, then I don't blame you for believing in global warming. Global warming states that temperatures are getting hotter because of greenhouse gases and man-made things. This theory is proven whether it gets warmer or colder. A tenth of a degree can be the difference between melting the polar ice caps and them staying ice. Then they throw all this technical mumbo jumbo like north-Atlantic wind tunnels or some crap like that to make it seem like they have a point. Can I definitively prove that theory wrong? No, I can't seem to find temperatures that stay the same to a tenth of a degree every year for 30 straight years, maybe there's something to this. Or maybe you've made a ridiculous point and need to stop pretending to be a scientist.

Just for the record, in the 1980s, people believed us to be in a global cooling and that we were bound for another ice age. What changed? Nothing really they just wanted to change it up.

In order for a good debate about global warming to happen, people need to take a stand either way. If your position is it's getting colder, I'll point to the record highs to provide evidence you're wrong. If your position is it's getting hotter, I'll point to the record lows to provide evidence you're wrong. Michael Crichton's book_*State of Fear* does a fantastic job of providing an argument against global warming but even he in the end admits that he has no idea if there is global warming.

Here's what I find when looking at data of temperature rising. In big cities, the temperature has gotten progressively hotter. In rural cities, the temperature has stayed pretty much the same. You only see J curves (when a graph is level and then shows a sharp increase) in big cities like New York, but not so much in Nebraska. This leads me to conclude that the fundamental problem with global warming is that it's not global. It seems to just stay in big cities. This is good for the people that argue for global warming, because most of the population lives in big cities so you can convince more people. I live in a very big city, New York, and I can tell you it doesn't snow nearly as much here as it did in Cleveland, Ohio, where I grew up. Cleveland is a decent size city, it's certainly big enough to have sports teams, so by normal standards it is a big city, but that can't keep the snow from falling because of the lake effect. These same experts that tell me that I, along with the rest of New York, will be washed away in a title wave, tell me that the Atlantic Ocean provides worse blizzards than a lake effect just not as often. After my seven winters in New York City vs. my 15 winters in Cleveland, I disagree. In New York, it rarely snows, when it does, it usually melts in approximately four days. New York was not always like this. In the 80s and earlier, it snowed a lot in New York, about as much as it does in Cleveland. Does this help the global warming theorists? Yes, I'd argue it does.

From a purely logical perspective, I just don't see how we can have global warming. The media and society tell me that the beautiful sunset I see is just the sun revealing all the pollution in the air. Then you read old texts of sailors talking about red skies as the sun falls. I believe that's a sunset is it not? Hundreds of years ago, they saw what I see now. How can it just be the pollution? Why doesn't the sun show the pollution in the daytime? Is it too bright? The more points they make, the more ridiculous the argument seems. I actually think man-made global warming is arrogant. I know we men believe we are destroying the environment and destroying mother Earth but I just look at nature and say no, mother Earth seems to do pretty well against us.

We have to continually make renovations because of erosion, water damage, the heat, the cold, high winds over time, etc. etc. If you abandon a building, plants start breaking through the concrete eventually and nature takes the structure back. Even when you don't abandon it, birds and wasps build nests on it. Yes, you can destroy them, but you're not really winning a battle. The birds and the wasps do quite well no matter what *Silent Spring* says.

Real quick aside about *Silent Spring*, the elimination of DDT in pesticides and crop dusting isn't what saved birds. All the book did was eliminate poor countries ability to effectively prevent getting malaria. The worse malaria gets, the more you can blame *Silent Spring*. Maybe developed countries can afford the alternatives, but developing countries can't. So they can't kill their bugs as effectively and they get malaria. If you bring DDT back, malaria will decrease. I guarantee it. (By the way global warming advocates, this is what's called a legitimate prediction because if DDT becomes legalized for 30 years and the malaria stays steady or goes up, then I'm wrong).

Furthering my point about global warming advocates being arrogant, I will point out that I'm just talking about nature in its every day calm sense. At its average, it takes back buildings, but what about hurricanes, tornadoes, tsunamis, earthquakes, and floods? One hurricane wiped out the city of New Orleans, which was also a big enough city to have professional sports teams. With all this constant maintenance because of wear and tear caused by nature, how can you declare we're winning? Also, people say that there are no trees. I have driven back and forth from Cleveland to New York many times and one thing I see during my drive is miles and miles of trees. In more than 20 years of being driven or driving back and forth between Cleveland and New York, I've seen no noticeable difference in the number of trees, so I'm not really too worried about that.

Recently I went whale watching in Boston. It was a week after I had returned from a trip to Croatia. Croatia, like Greece, has really clear water, which I always attributed to it not being polluted. Corfu is still the clearest water I've ever seen, seeing the bottom is absolutely no problem. When I see the waters of Greece and Croatia (Ionian,

Aegean and Adriatic Seas), I can't help but feel bad for how horribly Boston, New York and Cleveland treat their water. Lake Erie is the most polluted of all the Great Lakes. The Cuyahoga River has caught on fire three times. The Hudson and East Rivers are disgusting and when I'm in shallow enough water where I can stand on Long Beach on Long Island, I can't see an inch deep, let alone to the bottom. On my whale watching adventure, however, I learned that the fact I can't see the bottom has nothing to do with pollution, but minerals in the water. The more minerals and nutrients there are in the water, the more murky the water. Maybe that's why I saw whales in Boston but only extremely tiny fish in Croatia and Greece. More lies by common thinking. Maybe that's why Mark Twain said, "If you're ever in agreement with the majority, it's time to pause and reflect."

We dump a lot of things into the oceans, lakes, and rivers, but nature has a way of getting rid of it and cleaning it up or adapting to it. If you watch the Discovery channel, they'll go into caves in remote mountains where you'll find natural sulfuric acid. The most amazing thing you find is that there are fish swimming in the sulfuric acid. If they put the camera inside, it would melt instantly, yet there are fish swimming around. You're trying to tell me nature can't handle some chemicals and oil spills now and then? They've seen underwater volcanoes erupt and mollusks crawling around the magma that would incinerate us or any man made equipment, yet the mollusks are doing okay. There are trees that will not shed their seeds unless it's burned by fire and you want to warn me about forest fires? Without forest fires those trees would die. But don't worry, nature provides them with a forest fire if we don't. I hate to break it to you mankind, okay, I lied, I love breaking it to you, you're just no match for nature. Mankind has about as good a chance of beating nature as a 10-year-old has at beating Kobe Bryant in a game of 1-1 100 consecutive times in 2010 AD. I say the year so someone doesn't ask this game to happen when Kobe is in his 60s…then again, Kobe would probably still beat any 10-year-old when he's 60.

Global Warming proponents live on fear and confusion. They actually convince you that no matter what happens with the weather, they're right. Then if you call them out on this, they say, "Better to be safe than sorry, you can't definitively prove that it isn't so maybe you should believe just in case."

My final conclusion is I have absolutely no idea if global warming is taking place. I also see no danger in believing either side. There is no problem with recycling. The fact that people can use things you're throwing out to make new things is good. That doesn't justify scaring us into believing in global warming though. I am thoroughly convinced I will not be sorry for not taking action because we cannot beat nature.

American Education

As I look at the American education system, I have one question: "How can we be the greatest country on Earth when we have one of the worst education systems in the world?"

Now, for those conservatives who agree with me, I must say that home schooling is worse than sending your kids to school to be indoctrinated into believing America is a horrible country that has abuscd thc world, destroyed the Earth and can't do anything right. Stop home schooling your kids. Sure they will win spelling bees but they can't function in the outside world. Some parents prefer this because they want their kids living with them their whole lives, and I pity your children because the greatest way to grow up is to live on your own. Send them to school so they can learn how to socialize with their peers. That cannot be taught at home. I've debated a home schooled woman that got into one of the, if not the, most selective schools in the country, and she got mad at me because I picked apart every single argument she made because she continually and constantly contradicted herself. By all objective tests and standards, she is far smarter than I, but in communicating this knowledge into a logical argument, she was found wanting. If she went to school, I don't think this would have been a problem

The previous paragraph might be the only nice thing I say about the American education system. According to voter registration, teachers vote and support Democrats ten times more frequently than they do Republicans. I like to explain this by saying that Republicans actually leave the walls of academia and create corporations and become successful on their own, which is what school was supposed to do for you in the first place. I won't go as far as to say that teachers are afraid of going out of the real world and not being in the shelter of academia, but I have trouble arguing against that.

College is the worse culprit of this. I've sat in philosophy (called social foundations) classes at NYU that were one hour of why I hate Bush and 15 minutes of philosophy. The man's name is Professor Regan. If you have a child at NYU taking his class, get him or her out because they will not learn anything about philosophy. I understand most of the country disapproved of President George W. Bush when he left office, but few would agree with Regan when he told his classes that President Bush told the troops that he will not and should not pray for them. Bush then said that instead, the troops should pray for him. This is just but one example of the ridiculousness. When I asked him where he got this crap from, he gave me a list of websites but then told me if I had AIM or AOL on my computer, AOL, being the horrible corporation that it is, automatically blocks all these websites so you won't be able to access them. Between the years of 2002-2006 when I attended NYU, AIM and AOL was very popular. I took this to mean he's making it up, taking a chance that people have AIM or AOL installed on their computer. Just out of curiosity and a little bit of laziness, I realized that I had another class called "Prose Composition," which taught me how to write essays. The professor, who was a stereotypical hippy complete with sandals, loud colorful shirts and peace earrings, had told us that we had to cite credible sources when writing our essays and she would be more than happy to tell us if a source was considered credible. I gave her the list that Professor Regan had given me, and she came back with she was only familiar with some of them and none of them were credible enough to use in an essay. The ones she couldn't find, I believe were the ones Regan made up and used the AOL/AIM argument so as not to be caught. Unfortunately there is not only one, but numerous professor Regan's on every campus across America.

Most of NYU's professors are old and have been teaching there since the 60's. In the 60's, they considered themselves socialist, now they just got rid of the term and say "liberal." I'm not saying all liberals are socialists, I'm saying that the people who called themselves socialists are now calling themselves liberals. Why aren't they fired you may ask? Simple, because they have tenure. Who the hell thought of tenure? If you know you won't be fired, how encouraged will you be to do well at your job? You won't be. Fear of being fired is what keeps employees vigilant to find better and more efficient ways to do their job so they can continually impress their boss for more job security. Yes, unions help in not getting fired, but even with unions, you still live in this fear. Eliminate that fear, quality will go down. Hence, the horrible education system in America. We're being taught by teachers and professors who have absolutely no motivation to innovate, improve or teach more efficiently and effectively so they simply don't.

Around the world, at young ages, kids can tell you who the leaders are of the United States, England, France, Germany and many other developed countries. If you ask an American student these same questions, they won't fare too well. In fact, almost everyone I talk to is absolutely amazed that I can name all 50 capitals. It is not an amazing feat for European students to name the capitals of the countries in Europe. In China and Japan, Algebra is taught in third grade, three years before us. In every educational category, Americans get destroyed. The only pass I'll give them is in foreign languages because Americans don't need to know other languages as much as other countries need to learn English. Some may call that arrogance on British and American parts, but it is the way things are. To give you an example, in Greece, you have to be fluent in English, Greek, and French to work at a mainland McDonalds and Greek, English and German to work in a McDonald's on some of the islands. There may not be many McDonald's employees if America had those same standards, even if it were English, Spanish and Mandarin, or any three languages you want to insert.

With the exception of college, education works like many other things, you get what you pay for. Public schools are filled with indoctrination and far-left propaganda. To avoid it, you have to pay for private school. By and large, Parochial schools give children the best opportunity to go to the college of their choice, but when you look at the choices we have for colleges in this country, I don't know if that's saying much. From kindergarten through senior year of high school

I was in private school. K-8 was Montessori,,high school was Jesuit Catholic then on to NYU for the remainder of my education. Most people would consider that a good education, and they will point to NYU and the Jesuit Catholic school. As someone that went to all three, I point to the Montessori. I have written an entire essay about why I believe Montessori school to be the best form of education today. In interest of time, I will just say that it focuses on learning three things: 1) Time Management 2) Learning from your mistakes 3) Self-reliance. Since the point of education is to prepare students for the real world, are there any three better things to learn to accomplish this goal? Parochial school and colleges fail in this endeavor.

Harvard University is considered by many to be the best school in the country. In fairness to other competitors, I will say it's one of the best schools in the country. When someone says they went to Harvard, people believe them to be very smart and some will use that to convince people. The fact that they went to Harvard is the only thing I have ever heard a Harvard professor say that made them sound intelligent. Every other time they're in the news they're saying something absolutely ridiculous! I think Professor Gates is a little too easy.

If you don't know the story, neighbors called the cops because they saw someone trying to break into his house. It turned out to be him. He couldn't get his door open so he asked the cab driver to help him wedge something in between and force his way in. He then started screaming at the cops when they showed up and asked him about it, which is their job to do. As the cops were leaving his house, he chased after them yelling at them. The officer warned him he was being disorderly. He continued his tirade about how they only came because he's Black, and got arrested for disorderly conduct. To me, he made a fool of himself and deserved what he got. It's not hard to prove you live somewhere and it's not as Dave Chappelle indicates that the cops will beat you when they see pictures of your kids because they think you broke in and put pictures of your kids everywhere. He returned to school and told his students something along the lines of he now knows how easy it is for a Black man to fall. Even he was arrested and he's a Harvard professor.

Professor Charles Ogletree Jr. says that the subject of former slaves of the Cherokee Indians should be considered as citizens is a moral issue. Whether or not someone is a citizen has nothing to do with morality, it has to do with the citizenship laws of the country they want citizenship in. Switzerland has the strictest citizenship rules in the world. Is Switzerland the most immoral country? I would say they are not. Having been to Switzerland, I would say they have the nicest people in the world.

Professor Cox brought a cow on campus saying that it would save the Earth because animals and vegetables belong in the yard. So....... it's his ancient right. You can see my article on global warming to see an extensive description of my opinion of global warming. Leave it to a Harvard Professor to take it to another extreme. He claims that cows eating grass saves the planet. If it's that easy, then we have less to fear than I thought.

If you're wondering how I found the last three examples, I typed in "Harvard Professor said" into google and these were the first three unique professors (Gates had a lot of hits). This provides evidence to my theory that almost every time a Harvard Professor says something in the media, it's idiotic. To be fair, there was a fourth Harvard professor, Professor John Ratey that says when kids exercise, it is good for the brain because it increases plasticity, which can lead to decreased anxiety and increased ability to focus. This is actually something that sounds intelligent. I don't know if it's true but at least it's not obviously ridiculous like most things I hear from Harvard professors. Maybe there's hope for Harvard after all.

The more I hear Harvard professors talk, the more I believe that people who get into Harvard are smart, but it has absolutely nothing to do with the fact they graduated Harvard. I'd be really interested to see a test in IQ rates or another standardized intelligence test from when students enter Harvard and after they graduate. I'd be willing to bet they perform worse...but that would probably be true for any college given that I believe pretty much all of them are run by illogical, idiotic, extremely far left professors who are incapable of logic, reason or common sense, which is why they've spent their lives in academia because in the competitive and more objective real world, they don't stand a chance.

The scariest thing about American education is that it is continually dumbed down in order to accommodate people. This is a broader problem for other things in America, like women firefighters have to perform less strenuous tasks than male ones in order to pass. It used to be that if you went to college, you increase your chances of getting a job. Now, employers aren't as impressed that you went to college because almost everybody goes to college. At face value, this could be a good thing, but it would only be a good thing if people didn't lower the standards in order to admit more people. Government should not be rewarded for their value in providing a good enough education to students to meet the standards of college. I am not in favor of rewarding bad behavior. I understand that college professors are stupid, but if they were capable of keeping the people smart enough to get into college in the old days, they probably can now. It doesn't even end when you're in college.

Since schools try to encourage children to stay and actually graduate after they get into college, they dumb down the classes to accommodate all the people that got in because they dumbed down the admissions aspect. Calculus is pivotal in gaining a deep understanding of economics. The fact that at NYU, a respected academic institution, students can graduate with a bachelor's degree in economics without ever taking a calculus course or any classes in which you need to know what an integral is isn't right. This is indicative how low colleges have sunk in order to include as many people as possible.

AMERICA

I love America. Of all the places I've been and seen, there is no place I'd rather live at this point in my life. Now, most Americans say this. Hell, even Michael Moore says this but because of his actions and everything else he says, I don't believe him. Some may not believe me when they read this chapter. Keep in mind how I defined "love" earlier in the book. Love doesn't mean that there's nothing about the object of your love that you don't like, in fact, if that's true, it's not love. For love, you need to be passionate about every single thing about it. This is the love I have for America. This chapter is about the things about this country that drive me crazy. To quote the old business motto: "Innovate or die." These are some of the things America needs to improve upon and fix to maintain its number one status.

In this country we are drilled with the fact that we have freedom of expression. We are the land of the free: Freedom of speech, freedom of religion and freedom of expression. Unfortunately, we do not lead the world in freedom of expression. There are protests in almost every country in the world, they're not all killed. I wouldn't recommend trying it in Singapore, but you can protest in pretty much any country. Since our country is founded on Puritan values, there are just some things we can't express. In the movie *Eurotrip*, you see a commercial of two attractive women doing things sexually in nature and the commercial ends by telling you it's an ad for "Happy Juice." Somehow women being all over each other have something to do with the juice. The point of advertising is so the viewers remember the product. It's been years since I've seen *Eurotrip,* but I remember that commercial. I believe that commercial was fake, but in Europe, it is not uncommon to see commercials throwing sex or vulgar images in order to sell a product. A real commercial that ran in Germany was a traditional family with two young children getting in a car. The father turns on the radio and a song comes on and says, in English, "I want to fuck you in the ass" over and over again in a nice melody.

As you watch the commercial, the family in the car is bobbing their heads to the music giving the impression that they are enjoying it. If this commercial was in America, social services would be trying to take the kids away from the parents and the FCC would be calling the network. The commercial ends by saying in German, "Want to learn English?"

Immediately you understand what you're seeing. The parents don't necessarily condone the music; they don't understand what the lyrics are saying. Your previous conception of the parents vanishes. Maybe social services can hang up the phone now, and you remember the product. This is effective advertising that would never be allowed to run in America because of government programs such as the FCC.

It doesn't just stop with advertising. I went to a parade for Carnevale in Viareggio, Italy. If you're in Italy during this time, Venice and Viareggio are the hot spots for Carnevale in Italy. In Viareggio, there was a parade complete with many floats, most making political commentaries, including showing Burlosconi, the prime minister of Italy, upside down in a joker costume signifying basically that he's a joke. One float intrigued me the most because you would never see it America. It was approximately a 50 foot woman with breasts proportional to its size with large hard nipples. That is what I call freedom of expression. You can't tell me we have that here. Yes, people here can call the president a Nazi, but European countries allow that too. They have all the freedom of expression we have, plus more. They're winning in this endeavor, which is appalling to Americans since we should be the land of the free. Here you can actually be arrested for public displays of affection (PDA). If that were the case in Italy, they would need to put up an extraordinary amount of jails. For the record, the PDA in Italy does go extremely overboard but I still don't think Italy should make a law against it like we do.

In order to give you an indication of the difference between freedom of expression in Italy (You can pretty much insert any European nation here) and America, I will tell you how they reacted to the same stimulus. It was Super Bowl Sunday in 2004, the New England Patriots were battling the Carolina Panthers. This is a huge American event but there was a bar in Italy, where I was at the time that was showing it. Needless to say, there were no Italians in that bar from what I could gather. The halftime show featured Janet Jackson performing live with Justin Timberlake. Many of you know what will happen during halftime; Justin Timberlake will pull down Janet Jackson's shirt flashing everyone watching. Allegedly the other breast had something under the shirt and that was the one that was supposed to be pulled down, but Timberlake messed it up. Those of you who were in America know what happened. The FCC went crazy. Now, you can't do anything on TV anymore. A woman wrapped in a towel that then cuts to a scene of her feet and the towel dropping to the floor as she jumps into a football player's arms was banned. The commercial did not show any sexual areas, yet it was too much for daytime TV. Television would suck for months to come because nobody was allowed to do anything because of Janet Jackson's "wardrobe malfunction."

What happened the day after the Super Bowl in Italy? I was in a crowded bar so I didn't really see it when it happened live. Maybe I could go on the internet and see if I can find somewhere the government hasn't found first. My research would prove unnecessary. The following morning on the front page of *La Republicca,* the main newspaper in Italy, was a close up of Janet Jackson's breast. Yea, Italy really understood the need to not be so sexual so they told the world. In case you missed it, which most of them did because not many people watch the Super Bowl in Italy, here it is on the front page. If they had ESPN top ten plays, it probably would have made it.

Freedom of religion is another big thing about America. If America could keep freedom of religion for all religions then I wouldn't have much of a problem. Unfortunately, it really is freedom of religion for non-Christians. Remember, America was founded by Christians, and you're telling me they wanted Christians to have the least freedom of religion as everyone else?

I don't think so.

Every now and then you have a Muslim woman who protests because she doesn't want to remove her veil to teach a class or get a driver's license or something of that nature. They claim it's against her religion to remove her veil or to be seen without her veil by anybody but her husband. Many people cry crocodile tears for her and yell freedom of religion. She is not being persecuted for her beliefs. If you're going to live in a country, you have to follow the customs. If you don't like the customs, you simply don't partake in it. In America, we use driver's licenses as a form of identification. If you're driving a car, the police officer needs to be sure it's you and not your sister, aunt, cousin or niece. The face is the most unique feature of the human anatomy. In fact, some killers will take the head so as to make identifying the body extremely difficult. There are very few people I can identify by other means besides their face, which includes the hair. Therefore, if a woman is veiled in her picture, it is impossible to use that as a form of identification, which is contrary to why we use driver's licenses in the first place. If you don't like this policy, simply don't get a license.

Furthermore, in the Muslim culture, the woman is supposed to be submissive and obedient to the husband. Some Muslim cultures beat women if they are seen in public without a male relative or husband. If they're going for a driver's license, clearly they're trying to violate this part of their religion, so why do we have to suffer because they decide to break some rules but adhere to others?

We shouldn't!

Muslim women who want to operate a vehicle need to make a choice, remove the veil or don't get a license. I will remind you, freedom of religion doesn't mean that you can do anything in the name of religion. What if someone just made up their own religion saying that it is part of their religion to kill a small child, an adult male, and female every year? We would arrest him for murder. Freedom of religion means we can't *persecute* someone for their religious beliefs. Not being able to get a driver's license unless you take off your veil is not persecution. You can get the license, keep the unveiled picture of you hidden, like most people do anyway, and drive the car with the veil. If you crash, you're going to have to show more people what you look like unveiled through the photo. Better make sure you can see really well out of it.

The argument is weaker when you deal with Muslim women professors. If I were to make the argument I'd say that in the Muslim religion, the woman isn't supposed to work or be educated so she's already violating some traditions. She's picking and choosing again. I may point out that you're hurting more people than you help, which is usually my recipe to not do something. You're hurting all the students that have her as a professor since they can't understand her and you are only helping her. Then again, if we didn't allow professors to teach because they were hard to understand, we would have a lot fewer professors. Everyone has a story of a teacher they had absolutely no idea what they were saying because their accent was too thick. There is logic for why she shouldn't be a teacher, but I have less of a problem with it because you're not sacrificing American custom and way we do things here for someone's benefit. She's free to practice her religion but don't impede on us because you chose it.

For those of you who scream that it's unfair that Muslims have to make sacrifices and choose between their beliefs and adhering to local customs and traditions in a country, I will tell you that Muslims aren't the only ones. In Greece, seven years after someone dies, the grave is dug up and the bones are washed. It is part of Greek Orthodoxy, which is our religion. This practice is not done by Greek Americans practicing Greek Orthodoxy in America because the United States health board will not let us. They believe that it's somehow unhealthy to dig up corpses. They are probably right, but then again, people live a lot longer in Greece so this outbreak that would result doesn't seem to affect them. Whatever the reason, we are not allowed, and this is something that the church does. By not allowing this, you're not persecuting one person, but everyone who practices the faith. A lot of Muslims do allow their women to show their faces, it's only certain sects who don't. All Greek Orthodox people in Greece wash their bones after seven years. If we have to take it so should the Muslims.

This one example of the double standard brings me to the most common occurrence of freedom of religion: The public schools. Some will say that it's a grey area. On one side you have freedom of religion, on the other, separation of church and state. I told you earlier what I think about grey areas. Here's how we rectify the situation, either ban all names for God or allow all names of God.

That simple.

On September 12, 2001, kids at Westlake High School reacted differently to the events that happened the day before. Many cut out the front page of the *Plain Dealer*, the main newspaper in Cleveland, that depicted the second plane crashing into the tower while the other was on fire. Although the picture doesn't really call for a description, some kids elected to use their freedom of speech and religion with the picture. One kid wrote "We're going to get you suckers" on top of it and put it in his locker. Some kids wrote "Jesus saves" over the picture and many others wrote "Praise Allah."

The kid who wrote "We're going to get you suckers," got suspended because he may have offended people.

I call it free speech, but this is about freedom of religion, so let's try to stay on topic. Similarly, "Jesus saves," was ordered to be removed by the school.

What about "Praise Allah"? Perfectly acceptable. When officials at Westlake High School in Westlake, Ohio were asked why the students who had "Jesus saves" were ordered to take it down but not "Praise Allah", they were told, "You can't use 'Jesus' in a public school because of separation of church and state and we can't do anything about the Arab children because it's part of their religion and we can't infringe on their freedom of religion."

The Christian parents complained to no avail. If you can't see the blatant hypocrisy in this, seek therapy. To further prove the ridiculousness of this, Jesus is considered a prophet in Muslim texts, so he's part of the Muslim religion too. Maybe that's how the debate should have been formed. Actually, either all the Allah and Jesus remarks should have been taken down or none of them. Separation of church and state means keeping Muslim religion out of our schools too. Somebody needs to tell public schools this. The only justification Westlake High School may have is that they have to close school many times because people keep calling in bomb threats. It gets so ridiculous that the school started ignoring them after a while. Anyway though, Muslims do have a large history of killing innocent people and bombing things if people attack their religion. In fact, it's the only religion I know that will kill people because they took offense to someone calling them violent... kind of proving the point to me.

Alright, so I don't think America really is the land of the free but what else do I have against this country? We are a capitalistic country. I'm a big fan of capitalism. After all, I'm an economist. Immediately, I'm against tariffs and subsidies and believe in a completely free market. Anyway, I digress. That's a boring discussion and people will want me to feel sorry for the poor, and I'll leave that to someone who knows about finance and more about economics than I do. The main part of capitalism that I want is……. I want private property.

Some may ask what I'm talking about since they own a home so it's their house. Or they will say they bought a car, they have assets.

No you don't!

Every year, I have to register my car with the state. If I don't, I get fined. It's my car. The government should have no say in what I do with it. Yes, it would make it much more difficult for cops to do their jobs, but I want it to be all mine and I can do whatever I want with it so long as I don't infringe on other people's rights. If the state has no idea that I own a car, I'm not infringing on anybody's rights. It isn't completely mine then. Can you say I need to suck it up like I told the Muslim women earlier to do? Yes, fine, I will. No more discussion about cars.

Do you own a home? No, you don't. For those of you who don't believe me, what happens if you don't pay your property taxes that the house is on? They take your house. You didn't put it up for collateral. They just took it from you because you didn't pay a fee to the government to be on the land it's on. Well, what if I buy the land from the state? Can't do that either. You buy an apartment you have to pay a monthly maintenance fee. Can you just not pay it and if something breaks call a repair man like they do in houses? No, that's not allowed. I don't consider this owning private property. Can the cops walk on to the property and tell you to keep the noise down? Yes, they can enforce the amount of noise coming from your house too. By what stretch of the imagination can you possible tell me that you own your house, when the government can take it away if you don't pay them a fee in the form of property tax?

The repo man is a great indication that you don't own anything. If you own a boat and owe money, they take it. If you offer the boat or house as collateral to the bank for a loan, that's different, you can argue you have private property and still do that, but even if you've never bet your boat or house on anything, they can take it. By the way, I know everyone doesn't have a boat, but I made a promise that I wouldn't' talk about cars, so I went to boats.

If you think that we have more private property than other countries, you're wrong again. In Greece, my family owns an apartment. It has been in our family for three generations. Nobody lives there, but since it costs us nothing to own it. We keep it in case we go to Greece and want to stay there. I've been to Greece 11 times but I don't spend much time there because it's near Athens and all my cousins and family are in Southern Greece so I normally stay down there. There are no property taxes in Greece. If you own property, you own the land, the structure, everything, you pay the Greek government 0, that's private property. Furthermore, Greece isn't even close to the most capitalistic country… in fact, it seems much closer to socialism. Despite this, they still have private property, whereas we don't. Let's duplicate the Greek sense of private property in America.

DREW

It's hard writing about the deceased. As I start this, I know that I am not a good enough writer to capture who Drew was. These words won't come even close. In seven years, I do not know of anyone else who has tried the task, so I may be the best hope. It's unfortunate Drew doesn't have a Mitch Album to do him justice. Even if he did though, would the average reader believe it? Few people ever say bad things about the dead and only report the positive. When you hear about the dead, in the back of your mind you know that he or she probably wasn't that great. The thing with Drew was, there really isn't much bad to be said. Most of this chapter is taken from my writing about Drew shortly after his death. I contemplated using it as notes to write about him now but doing that would lose the emotion and confusion I had after his death. I want to get as much raw emotion as possible so bear with me as I will revert to present and past tense. To give a weak thesis statement on Drew, I would say he was generous, kind, compassionate, loving, religious and committed.

On June 7, 1983, the greatest person I have ever known was born. It wouldn't be for another seven years before I would have met him but nonetheless this is where his life started. The only thing I will mention during the seven years of his life I did not know him is that when he was two years old, he was diagnosed with chondrosarcoma, a rare form of cancer in his cheek. He responded well to treatment and was given a clean bill of health and able to attend school when he was three like others his age.

Oddly, I do remember the first time I met him. I was in first grade, he in second, and we were sitting in a circle as the teacher asked every student which fruit they would be bringing in for a class fruit salad. When the teacher got to me, I said "Peponi."

The teacher looked at me confused and asked me to repeat it several times, each time not understanding me. Then a boy in the class spoke out and said, "Cantaloupe."

I had never heard that word in my life. This is part of the problem growing up with two languages being spoken to you. You sometimes don't realize which word is which language. I approached him after the circle and asked him, "What the hell is a cantaloupe?"

He responded, "That's Peponi in English. Peponi is Greek."

"You're Greek?"

"Yes."

That is what sparked a friendship that will last for the rest of my life. The previous sentence is not a typo, Drew will always be my best friend regardless if he's breathing or not. Shortly after that, his mom invited me over to his house to sleep over. My mom was worried because she didn't think I was old enough to handle being away from home for an entire night without my parents. When the morning came, I didn't want to leave Drew's house and every Friday I would return to Drew's house to hang out with him when he was home up until high school.

Drew always wanted to help people. He acted as a psychologist for all his friends and he always knew the right things to say. It is a regret of mine that I was never able to return the favor. In fact, when he did get into some emotional problems later in life, he sought out professional help rather than his friends. It pained me that I couldn't be for him what he was to me but that is the way Drew wanted it. No matter how bad things got with him, he never wanted anyone to feel sorry for him so he always spoke in a calm and collected tone. If one were to pry, he would turn the conversation around to talk about your problems rather than his. A lot of people tell me that I'm good at giving advice, I got it from Drew. Every compliment I receive for my advice giving I credit to Drew. He gave me advice on my problems and how to give advice. Drew had a variety of friends as is evidenced by the amount of people that called others to inform them of the world's loss of the greatest person. He made time for each and every one of them. Not many people can get away with always being nice and considerate, they are usually the object of criticism, but Drew got away with it. That was the mystique about Drew. Drew was tenacious and accepting. There wasn't an ounce of hate in his body. Many people claim they are free of hate, Drew never did, he showed it through his actions. Although Drew disliked an extremely few amount of people, all were with just cause. And at the slightest instant if they showed remorse or explained themselves, they were forgiven. He never held a grudge and turned the other cheek at most every turn. Some Christians wear a band around their arm with the letters "WWJD" standing for What Would Jesus Do? If someone wore a band saying "WWDD" for What would Drew do? The two would be almost identical, or closest than if any other name is substituted. Drew was loyal. He kept all his secrets, a trait I thrive to mimic. He was an angel. He was truly a gift to the world.

Drew was an extremely gifted tri-athlete. He excelled in Basketball, baseball and football. He continuously worked out to improve his strength and would wear ankle weights in junior high school to improve his vertical leap, which worked amazingly well. I remember one football game of Drew's in which he was playing for second-last place in what is commonly called, "The toilet bowl." Drew would have two catches for 40 yards and 30 yards on an 80 yard field. On the 30-yard play, he actually ran up 10 yards to catch the ball before running back the other way for a large gain.

The shock that occurred on March 21, 2002 was unbearable. He and his parents informed me that there were miniscule amounts of cancer on his bone and all he needed was one shot every month. That's what the treatment was down to. I knew he didn't have the use of his legs, but his upper body still seemed strong. His explanation was that of the cancer blocked the main artery to the legs, and the shot was clearing it up. This sounds like a recovery story, but the harsh news came. After I heard, I refused to believe it so I called Drew's mom who answered the phone crying. She simply said, "We lost him" and thanked me for always being a good friend to Drew. I was too stunned to speak and mumbled something before getting off the phone and yelling at my family to leave me alone.

A few people called me, and I called a few people. I spent the majority of the night talking with people that knew him. While doing this, it occurred to me just how many people Drew touched in his close to 19 years of life. He attended Cavs games and school till the end. He fought cancer and did things he wanted to do for six years. He found a loving girlfriend in Yeketrina and great leadership in his parents. Drew was the best friend I have ever, or will ever have. He understood every situation, never had petty criticisms for anyone and a realist. There's an old expression that says, "It's the dash that counts," referring to on a tombstone that says the birth date to the death date and a dash between the two. It only matters what is done with that dash. Drew's dash was almost 19 years, and with his dash, he helped others, started a band, and maintained a great way of life.

How do you console somebody from this? I know how hard it is because I'm going through this at my grandfather's funeral, but I just talked to his girlfriend and I didn't know what to say. I feel like I'm fucking up, I haven't gone to see Drew's parents yet. It's just that I'm afraid, I don't know what to do. And I just feel like I'm letting my friend down. I know he's very understanding but I feel like I wasn't the friend to him I used to be. I know I tried with my phone calls to him that were rarely answered but I never got mad. I tried to show him the same compassion and understanding he showed me. He was always honest and told the truth. At first I believed that if I found out that he was bending the truth about his condition that I would be heartbroken and a little angry that he wouldn't tell me, his best friend. But I'm not. I understand why he did it because I understand him. He didn't want anybody to feel bad for him. That's why in his death, we should mourn, but still live life. I feel like I betrayed him. I feel disgusted with myself, I hope Drew can show me his forgiveness from heaven. He's a great kid I say "is" because he lives on in me and all he's touched. I saw him with tubes in him drawing blood and IV's but he never gave up spirit, and I was there for him. I wish I could have been there for him like that in the end. I'm told a lot of people feel like this when someone dies, but

I'm having trouble convincing myself otherwise. I'm going to find it easier to live by WWJD by asking WWDD because like I said their paths are virtually identical. I was very fortunate to have this close of a friendship. A lot of people go through life without what Drew and I had, and that's unfortunate. I will never forget it.

Yesterday (March 22, 2002) I went to Drew's house after we had a talk with our priest at our church where we spoke of memories so the priest had things to say at the funeral. The priest was not the same one we had growing up so he didn't know Drew very well. Our childhood priest did return to speak at the wake. There were a lot of his closest friends huddled in the basement talking about him and reminiscing about the days of old. I got back at 4:00a.m. from his house, and then I wrote an outline of memories I have that I want to include in this. It's weird having many memories back to back to each other but if I still have this a few years from now, I would hope that maybe I had forgotten one of these memories and this could remind me, and give me one last thing to remember Drew by. First, emotions.....I didn't cry at his house. I almost cried driving alone on the way home after dropping off two of Drew's friends. I did cry this morning when I thought that I betrayed Drew by not trying to draw out what he was feeling and just falling for the "Tell me about you" trick which is actually what kept him going.

Shortly before I left his house, we cleaned the basement. I was the last to leave the basement and when I shut the door, I just put my head on it. I probably have closed that door hundreds of times before but this time was different. It was like closing a chapter of my life. It won't be the last time I go into that basement as we are planning on going back today. After all night of talking about staying strong and Drew not wanting us to cry, it got to some of us. We all had a group hug and consoled each other. We tried to continue with saying Drew wouldn't want it but they knew that it was okay. It is okay to cry, so they let it all out. We were upstairs hugging Drew's parents good bye. Drew's mom cried and we had another group hug with her. Drew's dad consoled all of us as he remained the strongest but I'm sure alone it will get to him like it did with me and I'm sure it did with all of us. A mutual friend of ours and I started looking at a picture of Drew when he was young in a king costume for Halloween. In the background the song, "Can't Find a Better Man," came on. We ignored all other parts of the song and sang "Can't Find a Better Man," when it came on. Nobody can find a better man than Drew. I saw a picture on his first floor of him lying down and his last girlfriend lying down behind him. That's the picture of Drew I want to remember. The funeral and wake was closed casket. That is the way I want to remember Drew. I always said I wanted someone to cry on my shoulder and be there. I did it multiple times yesterday. It didn't make me feel powerful, it was right. That's what I recall about yesterday. As always, Drew's mom bought us some beer and there was food. Most people drank, I didn't. The last ones to leave spoke extensively on how upset they were that some people were not in attendance. I would always be over talked if I tried to say anything about this but Drew wouldn't have cared.

I went to most of his band's gigs. Including his first one where he dropped his pick and played with his fingers, which eventually cut and blood was all over the guitar and his shirt. He brought me together with a lot of people. I would never have known his last girlfriend, my first employer, or my first girlfriend had it not been for him. One of my friends would have been an enemy had it not been for Drew. The camaraderie between everyone that was in that basement was remarkable. Many people had multiple shoulders they used to cry on. Everyone was together to battle the travesty. It was good. So many people that he touched were there, not all, but a good amount. That's what we'll remember.

The following are some miscellaneous memories of growing up with Drew. At his birthday party we would play Ghosts in the Graveyard, which was just a fancy way of saying hide and go seek outside in the dark. Dan Fike's (a former Cleveland Brown's player that lived next door to Drew) house provided a plethora of hiding places. Every year his friends would play and then sleep over. Usually they'd all be dead tired and Drew and I would be wide-awake. Apparently one night, one of his friends was sleeping over and he fell asleep and me and Drew starting hitting him with Cavs pillows. I don't remember that but I don't doubt it either. I remember at one party he yelled at everybody to get up because they were sleeping too early and he said, "Except Larry who's hardly blinking."

I never did sleep. We would watch WWF videos, movies such as *Cannonball Run*, *Captain Ron*, and *Life with Mikey*. Drew loved quoting *Life with Mickey* and would tell anyone who was hyper to "Switch to Decaf" referencing that movie. There were many more movies watched, but those were seen many times. Other sayings he had were" Ladyodabed".I still don't know how he got that but it means what it sounds like. He also would make fun of the Cavaliers' announcers because we were die hard Cavs fans. He would say things like, "The Cavs battle the slippery Spurs from San Antoine" making fun of Michael Ragae. And then he would mimic the old announcers that couldn't pronounce Brad Daugherty's name. So Drew would say, "Dotty in the fore court passes to Price, Price to Nance, Nance back to Dotty, Dotty drop steps and scores."

Drew and I went to Brad Daugherty's house since he lived so close to Drew (about a two minute walk) one day. It was for an autograph for me. Daugherty knew Drew since his mom made him Greek food a lot. He answered the door and I looked up in awe. He had a back injury. It was shortly before retiring but he still was 7'1" and I was young. I asked him for an autograph and he yelled at me and then signed it. His exact words were, "I don't usually do this at my home, but I will this once, (sticking out his finger) but don't ask me again!"

I was too scared to disagree. The worst thing is, I lost that autograph. Then Shawn Kemp moved in after coming to Cleveland and Daugherty moved away. Drew and I would always ride our bikes through the woods and to the movie theaters during the summer. Drew always stuck up for me when the neighborhood kids would make fun of me. I remember him throwing one kid across the room. I say it's because he was making fun of me but I'm not really sure why. I do remember it was a good reason. It would have to be for Drew to react to ANY sort of violence. The kid wasn't even mad. We always knew which houses would give us popsicles. There were mountain bikers in the woods, and we watched them fall. Sometimes when nobody was on, we would ride over the hills, but we never jumped. We saw enough wipe outs and injuries to not try it. Drew usually addressed me, especially in his later stages, as "You sexy sexy man." That made me feel good since we both knew my lack of success with girls.

Like most Greek families, every time I slept over....or came over at all, Drew's mom would always give us food whether it be popcorn, chips or cheeseburgers. One thing I remember a lot is her saying, "Drew, do you want anything to eat? Larry, I'm making you a cheeseburger."

She didn't give me much choice but I liked her cheeseburgers and she knew that. Usually his dad would cook scrambled eggs and white toast for me, rye for Drew. Sometimes corn accompanied it. These late nights is what got me addicted to soda since I drank so much over there. Also, I watched Survivor Series 1990, which hooked me to WWF and the Undertaker. Now I look at that wrestler's name and cringe on what it means and the symbolism. And as much as we thought Paul Bearer was funny as a fat old man, I was asked to be a pallbearer for Drew and I'm honored.

Drew always taught people to be themselves. ...... Not worry what someone else thought of them. People regarded him highly and he had so many friends that nobody could touch him. I don't know anyone that ever stayed mad at him. This helped many people and even saved a girl in my grade's life. She contemplated suicide and Drew talked her down.

Drew always had a saying for me called "Getting the slobber going." This referred to when I would get extremely mad and lose my temper....... "Snap" for lack of a better term. I would get so enraged, I would drool like a rabid dog, so he told people that if Larry got the slobber going, it was all over. That brought a smile to everyone's face including mine. People still talk about how I never seemed to stay down and just kept coming, I hope next time I'm in a fight I can imitate this.

Drew was unquestionably very honest with people. He told people the truth, except with his condition at the very end, but in the stages he would say what the procedure was, but he purposely would undermine the severity of it.

His disease was cancer. There is so much horror behind that word. I witnessed it and if you ask me to describe the disease, I'll say it's a disease that literally frustrates you to death. Now what you must realize is that all this is based on what I know. Drew would try to withhold specific information so people wouldn't feel bad for him. There could be more to a story than I tell, I just don't know it. Late in his fifth grade year, approximately nine years after his first encounter, it came back. It all started when we were at recess playing a game of 500. In 500, a person is a thrower; he throws a football into a crowd of people and screams out a number from 1-500. Whoever catches it gets the amount of points the thrower yells out. The first person that gets 500 or more wins. If the thrower yells, "dead or alive" that means that the ball doesn't have to be caught to get the points. It could hit the ground and someone can pick it up and get the points. Drew was playing this game and the thrower threw the football and yelled "Dead or alive." The ball struck the ground and Drew dived for it. A kid a year younger than Drew also dived for the football and both his knees collided with Drew's cheek. Drew's dad was called and he took him to the hospital or somewhere to seek medical attention. That's when they found cancer. He would go on to miss most of his sixth grade year from extensive chemotherapy. During this time, I remember going to visit him in the hospital with another good friend of his. I believe there were more people but I don't remember who. When I saw him there were many IV's in him. I hated seeing my best friend like that. I would sleep in the hospital due to the fact I was so stressed out. Before I did, we had lunch with Drew. He had a little marker board where someone would write if he was in or out. So we ate at the cafeteria and talked with him. I challenged him to an arm wrestling match since he would always beat me at school. This may seem mean but with Drew he didn't want anyone to feel sorry for him, so I treated him like I would without cancer.

He beat me. Yes that's right, the kid had IV galore in his arms, blood being drained out, exhausted from chemotherapy and he beat me. The pathetic thing is,...... I was trying. When he was released I visited him alone. I brought him a nerf rocket, actually it wasn't the brand name "Nerf" but that's what everyone called it. Kind of like Kleenex, it just refers to all tissues. He put it in his brother's room. The site was something I will never forget. Again..... IV's in his hands and then a tube in his neck drawing out blood.

After a long grueling fight in which he technically did not attend enough days of school to go on to seventh grade, he defeated cancer for the second time. He then went through extensive radiation starting in January of his sixth grade year. I saw one of these. It was just him in a room with an apron on so the radiation beams are localized to a specific area. A big machine contorts itself to shoot it on that area, all leave room, zap, then rearrange it to hit another specific location. That's all I remember except for at the door there was a camera and he just said hi and they knew who he was.

The principal did let him go on to seventh grade, where he would have a full year of health competing in sports and living like a normal seventh grader.

On to the eighth grade the cancer came back. They caught it early. He went into the hospital on a Thursday he was out Saturday. I saw him and we had to wheel him around in a wheelchair. I didn't think he looked too good and I thought the doctor was wrong about Saturday. I thought it would be much later though I didn't tell Drew my theory. His grandmother agreed with me though. At the hospital I went to sleep. This is when I thought I was being a good friend.

Over the next four years, he had some surgeries here and there, scares, but cancer wasn't coming back until October, his senior year, when the doctors saw a cyst in his cheek. They couldn't see under it so they operated to remove it and check for cancer. Then they talked with him and his family and informed them that the cyst surgery would only take a few hours. Two weeks later, however, they wanted to operate again, and that one was around a 12-15 hour surgery. They said it would be the surgery to end all surgeries. They had to take bones from his shin to use for his face. The lead singer of his band offered to give up his bones but Drew refused. Had he needed it, I would have gladly done it too. I can name a lot of people who would as well. The first surgery was a success taking out the cyst. November was the big one. It happened sometime around the 14th. They operated, and checked things out, replaced bones and tried to seek out and destroy any cancer. They patched him up and gave him more skin to make his face more proportional. I visited him in the hospital twice while he was recovering from this. My mom came with me, and I saw his girlfriend there once and another friend with her the second time. He looked good. I brought him a sweater that I bought with my mom. He didn't get another surgery after that.

While talking about this surgery before it happened was the only time I saw Drew break down. We were downtown for a Cavs game and while driving he started telling me about it before getting choked up. It didn't last long but he showed how frustrated he was getting with all these surgeries.

Drew graduated high school and received another scare. He was told there may be some trace amounts of cancer in his spine. He traveled to the Mayo clinic in Minnesota. They gave him the latest technology of a shot that targeted the bones and washed them to try to see if bacteria were hiding in the tiny crevices. This would disable the use of legs but it may kill the cancer cells we can't see. After this, they sent the shot to the Cleveland Clinic, where all this treatment was done. He got it once a month. This caused him to need a wheelchair.

While in Minnesota, rumors spread he was doing very bad and bed ridden at the hospital. In reality, he was eating Italian food in his hotel room about to come home the next day. I know this because I was confused after hearing the rumor since I just talked to him. I called him and he told me. I yelled at the starters of the rumor. After that, a lot of adults at our church said that they wouldn't believe anything about Drew unless it was from me. His condition didn't make much improvement. He was at home except when he'd go to the clinic for the shot and leave. I believe this was a chemo shot. Then he got a cold and his immune system was too weak to fight it and he passed away March 21, 2002. They say he didn't have any pain because his disease affected his nervous system so he couldn't feel it. This makes me believe that these once a month shots were not preliminary shots to attack bones in case there's a cancer on them that they can't see. I believe it was widespread and he just didn't want us to know about it. Maybe the rumors had truth to them except he wasn't bed ridden in Minnesota. Thinking back on this time, I realize that if Drew had told me about his condition in its severity and told me not to tell anyone, I wouldn't have attacked people so vehemently. My justification would have been that they found out but I wasn't the one to tell them. Although this is a correct statement, it proves why he couldn't tell me. He needed me, his best friend, the one most people believed about his condition, to vehemently squash all rumors that he was doing bad. To do this, he had to lie to me.

When he graduated eighth grade, he gave a graduation speech like everyone did at our grade school. In his speech, he thanked me, and had a paragraph about me. I almost cried. The girl he had talked out of suicide held my hand. I was amazed that he was so loyal and good to everyone. He never made me feel sorry for myself and those times came often. We would make lists on the computer and he would put me as his best friend. I doubted it and thought that he changed it depending on who came over. How could someone as insignificant as me be his best friend? However, one of his friends told me after his death that he was jealous when he would see my name as his best friend. Thinking back on that time, I remember a kid I spent most my childhood hating saw it and mentioned his seeing me first. He kept it there. It was no trick but I still didn't think I deserved it. I didn't deserve to have a friend like him. I doubted it too much, and he proved me wrong at every turn. But the fact I doubted makes me undeserving. That's why it hurts so much that I couldn't get a hold of him. It hurts more that I didn't try every day but I keep remembering that when I did, it was as if nothing happened, like I talked to him five minutes ago. I also mentioned him in my graduation speech, but it was more risky for him to include me because others may have looked down on it, but they never did. You couldn't, that's the type of person Drew was, the exception. He was there for everyone.

During grade school, Drew and I would go to the Rocky River football games because his cousin played there. Afterwards we went to Michael's for dinner with the owner's son, who was a friend of ours, and got our food for free. Actually one time his son asked me a favor and I told him that I'd only do it if when we go to Michael's it's free. Then he told me it always was. I felt like an idiot for not realizing that before, but that's okay. During the games, we usually walked around and talked to people rather than actually watch the game. Drew wanted to go to Rocky River but he had moved to Westlake. Sometimes we even went to the away games. I remember one in Olmsted Falls because the kids there were nonstop fighting with each other. I heard one kid say, "You ripped my shirt, you're my best friend and you've ripped so many of my shirts."

I thought that odd, Drew and I had a lot of wrestling matches and other rough activities, but we never ripped each other's clothing. I went to more River games than my high school's when I attended there despite their winning the state championship two of my four years there and having probably the best high school football program in Ohio. Drew played football, so I think he understood what was going on more than I did.

Drew was kind and considerate, but if you tried to hurt one of his friends he'd be behind them in a second. I mentioned earlier when he threw a kid for teasing me. When an Arab kid our age and his brothers went to gang up on me, he helped me out to even the odds. He was a good fighter even though he didn't use it that much. One time, our friend's sister had a pillow over her brother's head and was pressing down, Drew shoved her off him. To this day, the brother says that he would have died had he not have done that. That may be an extreme but it goes along with how he always looked out for his friends. At a Greek dance, someone we knew from another church picked a fight with one of our friends, Drew, recovering from his extensive treatment, stood beside him and said, "You have a problem with him, you have a problem with me."

One punch could have severely hurt him, if not kill him, but he was willing to make that sacrifice for his friend. On one occasion I was with my mom picking up Drew from his house and I just heard him yell at a bunch of Arabs that were making fun of him because he was hanging out with a loser like me. Drew yelled at them to stop making fun of me and got in my mom's car. It wasn't always physical either. I lack a good vertical leap, and I couldn't touch his ceiling when jumping that I now can flat footed with my arms not even fully extended and still push it a few inches high. I remember where the six-foot basketball hoop is. I could touch that ceiling but not the lower one where the TV was, which is odd. He took me in his brother's room and asked me to try to touch the metal ring on the smoke detector because it was the lowest thing. I couldn't get it. Then he told me to go for the ceiling, I did and I missed. Then he realized that if I jumped like that for the ring, I would have hit it because my hand went above the ring when going for the ceiling. So he told me to jump for the ceiling but under the metal detector and I nailed the ring. It raised my self-esteem a little. It's stupid. But Drew worked with me to protect me against my own self-pity.

Football was the first sport he was forced to stop because of his condition. I think he played wide receiver. In baseball he was a catcher mostly but he sometimes played first base. I remember going with him to the mall to test out bats, (he could get a hold of balls.) Once at Clague Park, he hit it over Clague Rd, which is a significant distance for a high school player, let alone little leaguer. He had a cannon on his arm and could get the ball to second base quickly. He really liked one of his baseball coaches that was also a teacher at Westlake high school whose last name, purely coincidentally as there was no relation, was the same as my first girlfriend. He and his teammates long after they played for the coach would imitate him with some of his sayings. For example, "Bat mechanics gentlemen." Yelling, 'How ya doing today Mr. (insert last name)" at the top of his lungs. If you asked him the same question, he would say "Good to know good to feel good to be." Due to how often I heard this man imitated, I wanted to meet him. On one occasion, Drew took me to a game he was coaching and pointed him out. Every time I tried approaching him, I would make up some excuse for why I couldn't. To this day, I have never met him nor do I have any idea what he's doing. I talked about him in specifics because some former Westlake High School students will be reading this book and I want them to easily be able to identify who I'm speaking about and maybe pass along this book so that he can know how much Drew appreciated him.

He played baseball as much as he could in between the times when he recovered and his cancer kept coming back. The last sport he had to give up was basketball. I played on his team a few times. He played this up until the end with the Greek Orthodox Youth Association (GOYA), which is a sports league between area Greek churches. He talked about playing AHEPA (An extension of GOYA for people over 18-years-old) since he missed part of his last year in GOYA. He wanted to come back since he was going to college locally, but then his condition got to what it was. Basketball was his favorite sport. At least the one he talked about the most and seemed to want to play the most. He was an avid Cavs fan as was I. Drew had a gift in sports with coordination and natural ability. He had a high vertical leap, a strong arm and a solid build. This was what he looked forward to when he was recovering. Recreational basketball was a lot of fun for him. He won championships there, and in GOYA. One game he played with a pad in his chest, it wasn't really an IV, come to think of it, I'm not sure what it was. I do know that any misguided hit that landed there would have been a disaster. His hair had not grown back from the chemotherapy and the patch was something for his recovery. Despite all of this, he still played, because he loved it that much.

Drew and I always talked about writing a book. Occasionally, when over his house, I would mention I wanted to work on it but he would tell me not to. He wanted to do it in a few years. That didn't make sense to me because we may forget things a few years from now. It was supposed to be about the stuff he went through after one of his girlfriend's (Stacey) dumped him and he went out with his final girlfriend, Yeketrina. Bear with me as I tell the story as I want to fulfill one goal of Drew's right now by making it a part of a book. When I do, it will prove why I couldn't write a whole book about it. For those of you familiar with the story, I know the names are changed, I didn't forget people's names.

Drew met Stacey online. They talked because they both knew the lead singer of his band and she was interested in playing bass for the band. They talked and saw each other about once a month. Then at a Greek festival the summer of 1997, Stacey came with a friend. I was working the soda stand and she asked where Drew was. I didn't know. She eventually found Drew. Her friend didn't say anything to me.

Soon after that first encounter with me, Stacey and Drew dated. The next day, I found out that her friend liked me. Her name was Jenn. I remember I would dial the first six numbers and hesitate before the seventh. Usually I hung up the phone before hitting that seventh digit. A girl just told me that her friend likes me and I'm still nervous. Then Stacey straight up told me to call her. She convinced me when she told me that all I had to do was say one sentence and she would talk for fifteen minutes. Since I had two lines, (this was before cell phones), I was talking with a friend on one line and dialing Jenn's number on the other. The friend recommended that I start the conversation with "hi" and it worked. I thought Stacey was exaggerating that Jenn would talk for 20 minutes in response to one sentence, but when I called her, she definitely did most of the talking of our three hour conversation. After 15 minutes, my friend hung up the phone as I appeared to have the conversation under control. I didn't call Jenn every day, and Stacey yelled at me because that's in the rules so I called her every day and talked to her for over three hours. Stacey then told me to ask her out because she would say, "Yes." I couldn't say the words so I sent her an e-mail asking her out. How pathetic is that? She didn't have AOL so it took a while for it to send, meanwhile I just talked to her on the phone.

She knew it was coming. Then she got it and said, "Yes in an e-mail back and she also mentioned in the e-mail how stupid it was since she's on the phone and she can just say it there. Now, Drew and Stacey's best friends were dating while they were.

Drew would never cheat on a girl. He could get most any girl, but if he was going out with someone he never cheated. To bolster Chris Rock's point that women go to extreme measures to try to get taken men to cheat, on one occasion an attractive girl asked Drew to play the guitar for her. Drew was very good at guitar and loved to play it. The girl took off her top while he was playing and straddled him. Drew gently pushed her off and politely sent the girl home defeated. I have never cheated on any girl, and although I've had my own experiences to back up Chris Rock, nothing like an attractive girl straddling me while topless. I think that I would resist too, but I give Drew credit because that takes will power and a lot of self-control and he, like almost all men after age 12, was a very horny kid. He would also not kiss and tell.

Some time later, Jenn dumped me in November of 1998 in an instant message shortly after finally getting AOL. We would date again in early March 1999, but that was over by May. By this time, Stacey joined Discord, Drew's band. In total, I went out with Jenn for five months. We broke up because it was hard seeing each other. The second time we went out, I asked her out over the phone (he's improving gentlemen). We had our normal conversation and then she had to go and I told her there was one more thing I had to ask and she listened. In a split second, I finished the fastest, "Do you wanna go out with me?" of all time. She said, "Yes." There was no pause between the two speakers, thank God she saw it coming because chances are I mumbled it and she just said yes and it just happened to be when I finished. I hardly ever saw her because she was busy with soccer and other extracurricular activities. She dumped me over the phone. She gave me all the hints and tried to get me to say it. I tried to, but I couldn't and she asked me if we would just sit around until one of us said it. It was a joke, but I answered the rhetorical question with a yes, she then said, "I think we should be friends." Oh and the infamous, "It's not you it's me," phrase was used by her too, but at least before she admitted that it's cliché. For some reason, this break up affected me more than any other break up I've had. It took a full seven months to get over it and I don't know why. The first time she dumped me, I wasn't too bad, but the second time was horrible.

Drew and Stacey were on and off for a while. Then that summer when I was going to be a Freshman, Drew went out with Tess. That didn't last long, but it ended without any hard feelings, unlike Drew and Stacey's break-ups. Drew and Stacey ended up dating a final time after the beginning of his sophomore year. Yeketrina and Stacey were friends and were both over Drew's house frequently. One time they were both drunk, it was Stacey, Lead Singer, Yeketrina, Drew, and I. Yeketrina and Stacey ran around putting toilet paper on people. Lead Singer wanted to kick them out but it wasn't his house so he didn't. Later on that night, Stacey got really upset and Drew consoled her. Lead Singer was unsympathetic and still wanted her out of the house. Shortly after that night, Stacey dumped Drew on October 30, 1998. The next day, Drew went to Yeketrina's Halloween party and asked her out. I went as "Stone Cold" and met Lead Singer's girlfriend who was "Wilma Flintstone," I wouldn't see her again until Friday March 22, 2002, the day after Drew died. Drew asked her out in person, he figured it out better than I, and Yeketrina said, "Yes." Before I go on with this, Stacey and Jenn were both obsessed with these "Rules of dating." Drew and I joked about this a lot. Drew always said, "Where is this book? I want to see it? I want to read it so I know not to break them." Of course this was said with much sarcasm. Apparently this book really exists, but we didn't know about it.

One rule in this alleged list was that if someone goes out with a girl, the guy can not ever date a friend of the girl's. By dating Yeketrina, Drew was breaking this rule, thus Stacey was infuriated. This didn't only get Stacey mad, Jenn, and two of Stacey's other friends that were also friend with Yeketrina joined in. It started with hate e-mails. Drew wouldn't go online that much so when he did, he was bombarded with them. They called him every name in the book because they will boldly defend these "Rules." They put pressure on Yeketrina to drop Drew or lose them. Yeketrina chose Drew since she realized that what they were doing was wrong. I give her all the credit in the world for that decision. That takes guts to not give in to all your closest friends about a guy, but I'm probably biased. Stacey and her friends would barge into Drew's house uninvited since his side door was always unlocked. This act of rudeness didn't sit well with Drew's mom. Yeketrina was over for the majority, if not all, of these incidents. Just as this was beginning to get out of hand, Stacey and her two friends (Jenn didn't accompany them this time) decided to take it one step further… vandalism. They went to his house and they threw toilet paper, eggs and condoms on it. Then they took ketchup and wrote the words "Pay back" and "Revenge." Yeketrina was over when this happened and she and Drew helped his parents clean it up. The police came. Drew gave them Stacey's name but didn't press charges. When he got in, Stacey called him and apologized. Drew called her a bitch and hung up the phone. She called again and Drew's mom picked up and told her that she was getting tired of all this stuff between Stacey and her friends and Drew. That was the only time I think Drew has ever used the word "bitch" toward someone in a derogatory manner and not accepted an apology right away. Part of the reason he didn't accept the apology is because he didn't think, and I agree, that it was sincere. If she was truly sorry, she would have come and helped him clean up. Drew mentioned that to her. Jenn was the first one who got tired of these games. She finally e-mailed Drew and told him that she was sorry for everything and she was getting sick of this war. Then Stacey accepted that Yeketrina and Drew were together and stopped the war and when she did, Drew forgave her. Inexplicably, one of her friends continued it but she was alone. Drew thought about retaliating on the girl's house but never did anything more than beep the horn late at night by her house while we were driving around. Finally, even she stopped the war and Yeketrina and Drew went out in peace. There was only one brief separation between them. September, I forget the year, for some reason in September Drew would always begin to rethink dating. Even though Stacey dumped Drew, it was probably due to his distance in September. Luckily, Drew and Yeketrina started going out Halloween so they had almost a full year before his September doubting. I helped both Drew and Yeketrina through their break up. Drew wanted to see a psychologist that he could get for free. I tried to help him with it but he wanted the professional opinion. He was the best at advice giving, so if he needs it, he needs a professional I guess. During their brief breakup, at Yeketrina's request, I called Drew to talk about it with Yeketrina on the phone. I could hear her crying in the background but I continued the conversation. Then Yeketrina's mom got on the phone and Drew figured out he wasn't only talking to me. He hung up after saying, "Hi Yeketrina." I tried playing dumb when Yeketrina's mom came on but Drew's not stupid. We both apologized, Yeketrina told him it was all her fault since she asked me to but it wasn't. I did it because those two were perfect together. Despite my young age, I could sense the love between them and I told both of them this. I know they loved each other like parents should, which is why it killed me to see them apart. This may have been the only time in my life I was not on Drew's side. They did get back together two weeks after breaking up. Also during these two weeks, for reasons I still do not know, Yeketrina invited me to her house and I accepted. I didn't have my driver's license yet so I got to her house by some means I don't recall: Anyway, Yeketrina would end up asking me to leave and calling Drew to pick me up. Drew was out with a couple of friends and he obliged. As sketchy as this sounds, Drew knew that there was no chance in hell I would ever hook up with a girl he was dating, which is why he showed no ill-will toward me when he picked me up. His two friends, who didn't know me too well, had a different opinion that I could tell by their looks but they never expressed it to me. As a point of order, Yeketrina did not flirt with me in any way during my time there, we just talked about Drew.

As I said, they did get back together and went steady and the following September was the first one in a while Drew didn't get the feelings. At least he didn't tell me about them. They remained together despite Yeketrina leaving to college two hours way at Toledo and stayed that way until Drew left Earth. Their love will always endure, because love doesn't end, and it never dies.

Thank you for staying with me through that obligation and now I will go back to my memories of Drew. Drew loved to drive around and talk. He did this with a lot of his friends. Shortly after he got his license, Drew, Yeketrina, and I got in his car and he drove in the Metroparks, which is a large forested area stretching to all the suburbs of Cleveland. Because of the Metroparks, people consider Cleveland a forest city. I was bouncing all over the back seat because I did that a lot. I asked where he was going and he just told us he'd drive until the Metroparks ended.

We ended up in Berea, which is 45 minutes by highway from where we lived in Cleveland and then found our way home. We didn't go the way we came because that would ruin the fun of almost getting lost. We didn't get lost. We drove around, and we found Dover Center, which runs right by Drew's house and took it all the way back to Westlake.

Drew set goals for himself. He wanted to enter the music business with Lead Singer. He and Lead Singer definitely knew a lot about music. The thought of being a psychologist crossed his mind, but upon reading a document he wrote it states he wanted to join the music business. Both these ideas he expressed to me but always leaned toward music. I always told him that either would be good, because he knew a lot about music, but he also was extremely good at giving advice. He planned on majoring in business in college. He had talked with Yeketrina about marriage. The first time was fourth of July his Junior year (2000). Normally this kind of talk amongst 17-year-olds is unreal and naive, but with Drew, had he lived, I think it would have come true. Drew's parents were high school sweet hearts and I tend to believe in things repeating in the next generation. He told Yeketrina in 2002 that he was going to walk by her birthday on April third. On April 3, 2002, he was no longer wheel chair bound and flew to Yeketrina. He could walk, run, and do whatever he wants from heaven. It wasn't a lie to Yeketrina, just the obvious answer wasn't the right one. Shortly before her birthday, I had gone over to Drew's house and his dad gave me money from Drew's wallet when he heard I would be visiting Yeketrina at her college. I took Yeketrina and a couple of her friends out on Drew's tab referencing it accordingly. Had he still been alive April third, I think he would have gotten up and walked for an instant. Drew was a miracle to help people in almost 19 years. He did by instilling in us his philosophies and his power and spirit. Anyone that knew him is a better person from it. Drew had a future here on Earth after 18, but his future that he did not convey verbally came true on Earth. That future was to bring people together and help them through any times of trouble they have no matter what pain he has and to not let physical pain hurt them emotionally or stop them from doing the things they want to do.

On March 23rd, 2002, two days after Drew's death I spoke with his yiayia (grandmother), she told me about Drew's final day. He sent his yiayia upstairs because he said he wanted to go to sleep. His yiayia did, that's when he commanded his spirit with God. Some people say Drew's dad was the first to find him dead, but his yiayia said she was. They checked his vital signs and they got no response. His yiayia began hitting him asking where her baby went. I can't even imagine the anguish that overcame her and his parents. His yiayia shut his eyes for him. That's the way Drew wanted to go, in his house, without anyone watching so they wouldn't feel bad. Now he can watch down on us from heaven and comfort us when we need it. He can be with all his friends simultaneously. Consoling Drew's yiayia after his death is the single worst thing I have ever had to do. I hope to never do it again. I remember reading in one of my psychology text books that the loss of a child is the most stressful thing to happen to someone. The death of a friend was fourth. I have been unfortunate enough to have to console two mothers in the loss of their child, and it is not something I want to have to do again. Neither experience, however, was as bad as seeing the anguish in Drew's yiayia's face as she told me the story. It didn't even resemble a human. She wasn't even looking at me. She stared in the distance and spoke to me in Greek since her English was passable at best. I had to console her in Greek, which made it that much harder. I still get chills when I think back to how she looked and sounded on the couch as she told me the story of finding her grandson dead. I know it's selfish, but I hope I never have to experience that again.

On a happier note, we had gone to Cedar Point in 1992 with his family. Cedar Point is consistently voted the best amusement in the world and is located in Sandusky, Ohio. If you enjoy amusement parks, go to Cedar Point. We were in a suite but I don't remember it being that nice, but on return trips the hotel looked nice. One night, I wet the pull out bed. Drew told me that someone probably poured water on it or it was the people before us. I don't know if he knew, but he probably did. I mean I was eight years old so I shouldn't be doing that, it was highly embarrassing but even then he didn't want me to feel bad about myself. He was watching the Dream Team win the gold medal in basketball. I didn't watch because I believed I was bad luck and they would lose if I watched. Big mistake, but that's okay. Cedar Point was fun as it always is. That wasn't the last time we would go. His eighth grade year, we went and got stuck on the top of the Magnum, which at 205 feet was the tallest roller coaster at the park at that time (now it's fourth in the park). Drew looked over and saw the beach and exclaimed that he saw a postcard of this same view. Maybe someone did take a picture at the top of the Magnum. This comment lightened the fear we all had about being stuck. He almost lost his hat twice on it during that trip, the first time the guy behind us caught it, the second time I caught it. Drew would always promise we would ride the big three at that time (Magnum, Raptor, and Mantis). Sometimes I doubted, but we usually did all three more than once.

Drew's death brought the end of an era. The era may have only lasted almost 19 years but he gave us lifelong memories. At his wake, there were many people that showed up. I consoled a lot of them and stayed strong until I was at his casket talking to him. I felt once again that I betrayed him and I cried. A mutual friend put his hand on my shoulder and I hugged him and dug my head in his shoulder. Then I stopped. It lasted about 10 seconds, and I thought of the time when he broke in front of me. He was driving so he couldn't dig his face in my shoulder but he gained composure like I did. At his wake, I saw some people I haven't seen for a while like his cousin. We were all brought together. Unfortunately, it had to be at a wake. In the Irish culture, wakes are celebrations, but this was more appropriate. You talk about the memories, celebrating doesn't seem right. I do see their argument that he's not in pain. He's with God so we should celebrate for him. It brought his mission to an end. His legacy is shifted to his friends to carry on. I started carrying it on while he was still alive as I would go to him for advice on how to give advice. Now in his death, I shall try to continue it and I know he will still be helping me. I hope I can know what to say to people in pain like he did. I know he will be with me now forever. Will I see him in heaven? I hope I get there.

I recall the week of March 18 – March 22, 2002 very well since it is the worst five day stretch of my entire life. On March 18, my Pappou (grandfather) died, which caused me to cancel my trip to the strip club the following day as I was turning 18-years-old and postponed it for Friday the 22nd. My parents tried to have a birthday for me on the 19th, my birthday, but I wasn't in the mood for celebrating my birthday as my grandfather had died the day before. The 20th was my grandfather's wake. March 21 was the worst day of all. It snowed heavily in Cleveland and I spent the morning at my pappou's funeral and burying him. Then my family went bowling to try to take our minds off it. When I got home, I watched *WWF Smackdown* as it was on Thursdays in 2002. The viewing was interrupted when one of my friends called me since he heard Drew died and wanted to make sure it wasn't just another rumor about Drew's condition that had been going on for months (which I believed were false). As you should know, it was confirmed. Friday, I then commiserated with Drew's friends and family at his house about his death. On Tuesday earlier that week, my birthday, I called Drew and told him about my grandfather's death, he expressed his condolences but ended the conversation quickly due to his exhaustion. The last thing he ever would say to me was "Happy Birthday." At that time, I should have known the rumors were true. He had never forgotten to call me on my birthday nor not helped me through a problem because he was too tired. I should've known that it would take an extraordinarily amount of pain to make him do this. I know hind-sight is 20/20 but that doesn't help me get over this.

On a happier note, I'll talk about Drew's siblings as they didn't get much attention in this. I remember when he first told me about his adopted sister. The year was 1995 and we were outside shooting a basketball around and he told me they were adopting a girl in a few months. She was going to be seven. I thought, and still do, that it was remarkable how Drew's parents could have one kid with cancer, another with autism, and find it in their hearts to adopt another kid with Fetal Alcohol Syndrome (FAS). I guess Drew's mom wanted a girl, I never asked but that's my assumption. Drew loved his brother and his sister very much. He always glorified his younger brother mostly about how strong and big he is. His brother is also very loving, which you can tell by his mannerisms. People say autistic kids are incapable of emotion, that's not true with Drew's brother. I don't really understand the term "Autistic." There was a kid that claimed to be autistic in my high school but he could talk and keep up in a college preparatory Jesuit school. Drew's brother couldn't even talk. I see what people call autism today, and it can't be the same word to describe what Drew's brother had.

There was always love between Drew and his sister. Drew always helped her with her homework and to feel happy about herself despite everything she had gone through in the seven years prior to living with his family. He always wanted his brother to recover by some miracle and to hear him talk even if it was only one word. I hope it happens now. The family needs some miracle and relief. Then again they have the same ones I do: Drew, his legacy and his message. That's very good relief. Still......

I hope now that Drew's in heaven he will help his brother get better and ask God personally. His sister is blessed to have such a loving family now. She was abused as a baby and now she has loving parents who take care of her. God bless Drew's entire family. Hopefully his sister remembers Drew's legacy and it gives her strength like it does me. I keep talking about his legacy, I hope everyone that knew him can remember it, live it, and find comfort in it.

"Discord" was a great experience for him. I made shirts for the band, unaware that band members aren't supposed to wear their own shirts. Drew gave his to Stacey, got it back and then to Yeketrina. I hope she still has it. If not, I don't take offense. Drew wasn't an original member of Discord as it was started with Lead Singer and two of his friends. The guitarist was kicked out, Drew joined as new guitarist and they started. The guitarist went on to form another band called the "Mad Ups" and tried to be the rival band. Drew, Lead Singer, and Original Drummer were the core of the band. The bass oscillated from Stacey to another of Lead Singer's friends. Their first performance was at Original Drummer's sister's graduation party. Stacey's amp was off and Drew played the bass part on his guitar. When they replaced Stacey at bass, they tried having her play keyboard but that didn't last long. He sat down during one song because it was sad and it added affect. Although his back was to the crowd, his guitar teacher told him it was a good idea, but to face the crowd. From then on in, he did. Then they played at Xanadu located in North Ridgeville, which is the next city west of Westlake, a few times. Despite it being a teen club, the atmosphere was smoke. Drew's dad taped some, I got to second base (up the shirt) for the first time at one of his gigs there. I think I went to every gig they had there even when the club's ownership changed to Teen Madhouse. After the ownership change it was owned by strict Christians who outlawed smoking (atmosphere changed), kissing, fondling, etc. Drew broke those rules with Yeketrina on multiple occasions. They moved on to Odeon in the Flats (downtown Cleveland), Rocky River Municipal Center and Earth (also in the Flats). They were strong the first two years of high school but practices became fewer. They would have them at the drummer's house but he started losing interest in calling practices and they declined. Lead Singer says that Discord died with Drew, which I think might be appropriate but Lead Singer should continue to play the guitar. If Lead Singer went on with a band, I don't think it would be bad, so whatever he decides I don't believe it will disrespect Drew. I remember one of his Indian friends and the girl he talked out of suicide were always at the Xandu gigs. They were fun. I went to almost every one. Some I missed because I was out of town, always for a good reason. I almost missed one because I got lost trying to find Earth, but I caught the last one or two songs. I had to call Drew's dad for the Odeon directions while I was downtown.

This is March 29, 2002. The funeral was four days ago on Greek Independence Day. The day the Greeks won their Independence from the Turks is also the day we buried Drew and now he's independent of cancer and pain. I got to the church at 12:30. Snow fell fast the entire day, making the roads very slippery. I believe this means that the world is cold without Drew. I put Drew's guitar on the stage in the church then went back outside to take the casket from the hearse to the church. Since I was the only pallbearer present, the two funeral directors and I carried it. Luckily it didn't go too far. Going into the church, the rest of the pallbearers showed up. We sat in the first pew and waited for the funeral to start. As we all listened to the funeral liturgy, one of us cried intermittently. Lead Singer shed some as well. I then realized that seven people were sitting in the pew for Pallbearers. The priest gave a great eulogy as he usually does. Some of the speech was recapping what we said about him at church the day after he died. The three things were how he helped people through problems and always said 'I'm fine, how are *you?*' showing his unselfishness, Drew the peacemaker, and ended with the story on how he saved a girl's life by talking her out of suicide. Then it was time for everyone to come up to venerate the casket and icon. During the final blessing they opened the casket, but turned it so the lid blocked the view of the body. If I was sitting on the side like I had been originally, I would have seen the body but they had called the Pallbearers to help shift it around. When we re-filed, I was in a different spot. Maybe Drew didn't want me to. That's what my mom said but I don't know.

While editing the writings about Drew to flow for this book, I have wrestled with whether or not to include the following story in the book. On one hand, I do not really want people's opinions of it, but on the other, I wanted to try to give full disclosure on the events following Drew's death. Before the wake, Yeketrina told me that Drew's dad invited her to see Drew's body before they closed it for the wake. I was jealous that I wasn't extended the same invitation. So much so, that I went to Drew's dad and expressed how I wanted to see his body if that was at all possible. He then extended the invitation to me. I didn't tell him that I knew of the showing before the wake or that Yeketrina was going. I knew I was forcing an invitation but I thought that's what I wanted. On the day of the wake, however, one of our mutual friends and Lead Singer called me asking that they wanted to go to the wake together. I knew that I couldn't say yes to them and see Drew's body at the same time. I couldn't think of a good excuse though as telling the truth was not an option. Ever since it happened, we had talked several times about how Drew wouldn't want us battling it alone but to be there for each other, so that didn't seem to work either. I agreed to pick them up and go to the wake when everyone else would. I didn't have Drew's dad new cell phone number. He didn't know I wouldn't be coming. At the wake, he said something to me about it as he tried to keep the casket open a little longer thinking I'd be coming but then he was forced to close it because people had arrived. Writing this over 7.5 years after his death, I still don't know if I made the right decision. Like I said earlier, I want to remember Drew by that picture of him lying down next to Yeketrina as they're both dressed in white. I will never know if seeing Drew dead would have changed that.

At my grandfather's funeral, the funeral directors had the pallbearers go up first... then they stood to the side as the rest of the church went up and they formed a wall when the family went up last. For Drew's, they told the pallbearers to remain seated. We couldn't even venerate the casket. People filed up to the left of the casket if you're facing the altar. The line was very long, then I saw the end and nobody was coming up. I began thinking that a lot of people showed up since the line was long but when that line ended, I realized more people coming from the right side. The people I had just seen were only half of the people present. This was very time consuming due to the amount of people there thus further strengthening my belief that Drew touched so many people. That never ceases to amaze me. As the people came up to venerate, the pallbearers all held hands. We weren't asked to, we just did. When Drew's yiayia went up, she stood at the casket and broke down crying. Her body was weak and she didn't want to move. I began thinking to myself that the pallbearer wall would've been good right now. But this funeral company didn't agree. There were no flowers in the church. I still don't know why nor will I ask Drew's parents because that wouldn't be appropriate. When everyone was finished showing their last respects, the pallbearers went up to carry the casket out of the church. I went up to it, and put my hand on it, bent over and kissed it. Now I could pay my last respects. The other pallbearers did the same. Then I turned around and looked out in the crowd for the first time. The church was jammed packed, I had some indication by the amount of people that came up, but all the pews were filled. Drew was simply amazing to touch all these people. That isn't even all of them either. It was like Easter Sunday when everyone shows up for that one time. We then carried it down the step and on to the holder. They wheeled it out and we carried it to the hearse through the blistering and heavy snowfall. My older brother drove since he was the best driver and we needed that because of the snow. I offered, but they gave me the front instead. We then drove to the cemetery very slowly due to the inclement weather and the custom with funeral processions. In the car, my younger brother said that Drew tried to be a peacemaker between me and him but I ruined it. This angered me, but I didn't say anything because this day, I was going to try to not show violence. When we got there we had to wait for the hearse. Finally it came, the pallbearers filed in behind it awaiting the casket. The funeral director told us that if we were going to fall, let go of the casket. The slick headstones of the departed in Lakewood Park Cemetery when wet are easy to slip on. While walking I felt bad because I kept stepping on the pallbearer's heels in front of me. There were four on my side and three on the other. My head was down due to the heavy snowfall and I slipped on two headstones and gave a short yell each time. I then voiced that I just hit the two, and hit two more and counted three and four as I did. Later, one of the pallbearer's would voice that this angered him since it was supposed to be a ceremonious walk to the grave and I shouldn't have been talking for those five seconds it took to say it. Lead singer agreed with him but I do not. Drew, and everyone else there, should know I meant no disrespect nor do I think it is even that disrespectful. We got to the tent and placed him on the holders above the casket. There were some flowers and two wreaths by the grave. My mom pointed to her head to remind me I had a winter hat on. I took it off and put it between my legs because the pallbearers were joining hands again. At the beginning when I was supposed to do my cross, I let go. I felt kind of bad because I didn't know which to do, break the hands and do the cross or keep the link. The other two Greek Orthodox pallbearer's did their cross too. I decided that I would remake the link of hands after. The priest seemed to be doing it quickly to get out of the cold. I don't blame him, but maybe we should ask the humanitarian and judger of right and wrong (the guy who initially yelled at me for talking during the walk). That was a little uncalled for. I'm sorry, back to the story. My hat fell to the ground somewhere in there and I didn't dare pick it up. At the end of the internment service, I did my cross and kissed the casket a couple more times. We all stayed around but made our way back to our cars. My brother knew a shortcut back to the church and took it. We got there before anyone else that went to the funeral. Some people told me that by the time they got to the cemetery, the service was over. That doesn't surprise me. His cousin tried to push the round tables together so all the kids could sit close to each other. It was a good idea but not much success came from it. Four tables were pushed closer, but not together because too many seats are lost through it. We talked and here is when I was reprimanded for speaking while carrying the casket and that he almost punched me for it (yea, that would have been much more respectful). I think many of Drew's friends look down on me. I don't know why that bothers me. Maybe I wish for Drew's sake, we all got along. Or maybe it's selfish and I want to be liked by more people. I mentioned how I was mad at my younger brother for saying that, and the Reprimandor told me what I already thought...... Try to not hate him for Drew.

After dinner, the principal at Drew's high school gave a speech about Drew. He talked about how Drew and he had a thing that if they saw each other in the hall, the principal would put a thumb up as a way of asking how Drew's day was. Drew would respond with a thumb up for a good day, thumbs down for a bad day or thumb sideways for a descent day. I couldn't see Drew giving a thumb down and I wasn't even sure if he would give a thumb's sideways either. The answer was, it was always a thumb up except once, when it was a thumb sideways. I wonder what happened on that day, I assume it's when he and Yeketrina broke up in that September time. But that's a guess. Then the friends went up. His cousins that are my age spoke first. They spoke to Drew rather than about him. The Reprimandor took the lead to picking who would speak because he wanted to go last. I went next and just said things off the top of my head. I talked about "What would Drew do (WWDD)", and how I realized how many people he touched. I ended by saying how much I don't think I deserve having him as a best friend. I guarantee someone thinks that I'm doing that as an act, but that's okay. I'm writing this with so much emotion because I love Drew so much, but hate vibes are filtering in because of things I *think* people think. I don't know what it is. I will just try to end all this by saying this, I don't care what anyone thinks, I know and Drew knows how much I loved him and that everything I say is not a ploy but completely sincere. When I began the speech, I said I didn't want to write it down so it came from the heart. Then I thought that the people before me read what they wrote so I tried covering by saying that if on paper, it's still from the heart, but I stopped it before I dug myself any deeper. While speaking, I realized I was talking longer than I planned so summed it up and ended with "Drew, I love you." Then I read a poem that one of my friends who knew Drew but never hung out with him wrote. Many people spoke. Some aspects I failed to mention in mine, one of the other speakers picked up. I'm glad I didn't say everything. Yeketrina didn't say much because she doesn't like speaking publicly. One pallbearer gave a good speech, first thanking and leading a round of applause for Drew's parents. The diner owner's son talked about how Drew or his mom would convince his parents to let him stay over when his parents said no. The Reprimandor talked about how much Drew liked to drive down Lake Road. I don't know if that's the road we drove down all the time, but I never pay attention when someone else is driving, so it probably was. I do remember when I sensed Drew was taking me home I faked sleep so that the conversation would go further with him and Yeketrina. Basically, I wanted to spend some time with Drew even if I was pretending to be unconscious. Drew would do donuts to wake me up. Eventually it was either start laughing or get up and let him take me home. It was always painful to go home after seeing Drew. All the speeches were heartfelt. The speaker who is the best writer of all the speakers read an essay he wrote about Drew. He cried in the middle, and the Reprimandor and me put a hand on his back as we did to anyone that got emotional since we were right by the mike thus behind the person speaking. Drew's uncle was the last person to speak and gave a good speech. Then we all huddled and sang "The Long Road" by Pearl Jam, like we all practiced and planned. Lead Singer played Drew's guitar and sang in the microphone. He had printed up the lyrics before and gave it to all of us to sing along. The person I shared the paper with started to cry in the middle. I realized he had a firm enough grip that if I let go, the paper wouldn't fall so I let go and put my arm around him. Pearl Jam's *Long Road* would never be the same for me after singing it that day.

Afterwards, people were leaving. Drew's cousin came up to me and told me I gave a good speech. I thanked him but thought it may have been routine. I noticed I said "like" a lot. Then he said to me, "I didn't see Drew too much, but listening to all these speeches by his friends, I know he was in good hands."

That meant so much to me..... His cousin trusting us to take care of him. I thanked his cousin again because that meant infinitely more to me than saying my speech was good. Many people said I gave a good speech, I thanked them. And I told the people who gave speeches the same. I found Drew's sister, whom I barely recognized because she grew so much. She was talking to her uncle so I kept my distance until she was finished, then I went up to her, and she was smiling. I envisioned I would be consoling her. Then she said to me, "He's not dead, he's alive in me"

I was so happy she understood that. I told her, "That's exactly right, he'll always be in your heart, in my heart and in all his friend's hearts, and we can still talk to him. He will never die."

Lead Singer and a girl he knew were going to a movie. The girl was thinking back on how she didn't say anything in her speech but just cried. I put my arm around her and told her that although the speech was short, the emotion was known. Drew knows what he meant to her, Drew knows she loved him and everyone else does too because somebody doesn't cry over someone as an act. I don't think it made her feel better but I hope it did a little. I mentioned the movie. Yes, I was inviting myself. The girl took my number, and I got hers too and she said she'd call me in an hour. On the way home, my mom told me that I had to take a piano lesson so couldn't go to a movie. The girl did call and I told her, she was a little surprised that I was having a piano lesson. I hope she knows I wasn't lying. I went to school the remainder of the week, and got caught up as I missed three days for Drew's death.

A petty thing that bothers me is Drew's final resting place. The cemetery he's buried at does not allow tombstones. I know from the plot my family has, a tombstone can be decorated much better than a headstone. Drew's dad did a good job designing Drew's gravestone as it has a picture of Drew's face, a basketball player wearing a jersey from one of his teams along with a football and mitt to fill the three sports he played. It has his birth date to his death date and his name is written with the nickname "The Drew Man" in between his first and last name. I can't think of a better design but it would be much cooler on a tombstone. The main thing that bothers me is that visitors are not allowed to leave anything on the graves. Something I put on my grandfather's grave when I was in fifth grade (The one that didn't die three days before Drew) is still there to this day (2009). When I put flowers on Drew's grave, the next day they were removed. For what would have been his 21st birthday, I brought him a beer, they took it away. My only act of rebellion is the unedited version of my memories of Drew I buried in his gravesite. Although I know it's possible that the elements could have dug it up and then they threw it away, I want to believe it's still there. Others of his friends have expressed their displeasure that when they leave personal items that can't die or go bad (like flowers) they take it away. Me and another kid made a pact to try to keep Drew's grave the best decorated but that's impossible since they just remove it every day.

For another example of Drew saving me from myself, I made a shirt with the words, "I'm the strongest kid in my grade" on the front, and on the back, "Don't mess with me." What possessed me to make this shirt is beyond me. Naturally, since I'm tall and lanky, I got a lot of criticism for it. But when people heard Drew praise it so strongly, the kids in my class stopped criticizing it. Instead of outright criticism I got constructive comments like, "If you change it to, "Toughest," then it might be true." Then people began figuring out who was the strongest kid in my grade. The point of this story is that when I did something stupid, Drew defended me by extolling it and since he had such widespread popularity people didn't go against him. That shirt was stolen and given away by my sister to her friend so it is no longer in my possession.

On December 31, 2002, I officially was the same age as Drew when he died. I was in Cleveland for the holidays but I drove up to stay in my dorm in New York as I wanted to be alone. I didn't tell anyone why I went back to New York for New Year's Eve. It was unseasonably 60 degrees that day and I was in Times Square by myself with a million other people. Since they block everything off, I had to get there ridiculously early and occupy myself standing in the same spot for eight hours. When the ball dropped signaling New Year's Day, 2003, I dropped my head. Every day from that day forth would be one more day Drew didn't get in his life. When the ball dropped, I lost my fear of death. Objectively, I don't deserve to live longer than Drew. I was in Times Square because it was something I wanted to do but my parents deemed dangerous. I was ready to die that day as I still am. Ironically, this lack of fear of death has allowed me to live life to the fullest and not get scared of experiencing or doing something just because I want it. Although there are still items on my bucket list, I can die in peace but I would never commit suicide.

Drew was a saint, mentor, and a friend. He was a saint in that he never complained about himself. He always prayed for other people and never for himself. I prayed for him, I pray for his soul now and for God to allow him to give me guidance and have him be my guardian. He had great faith in God. That's what gave him hope no matter what happened. It gave him some of his strength. He helped other people, and gave them strength, made them happy for being who they are. Seeing Drew with tubes and so weak was stressful, not depressing because he lifted my spirit and I realized that cancer wasn't stopping his way of life. He got strength through helping others. That's what made a difference. A man who lives for others is a saint. He didn't publicize it so he won't be canonized, but why publicize? He carried out his mission. It didn't matter how many people knew he was doing it. This is also what made him a mentor. He guided you in life whether it be in academics, athletics, girlfriends, or life in general. He guided you down the right path, and was always with you in good and in bad. This is what made him a friend. A friend is someone that you can always rely on, that never leaves your side. At first I didn't think I fit that definition since when I lived 15 minutes away, I didn't see him. But I called him, and I was always by his side in spirit. If he ever needed me, I always came.

This is my best friend Drew Bliss. There are some memories I didn't list just in case someone reads them and it was to be between him and me. I will always miss him and love him. He was my mentor, friend, and now guardian. I hope I have the strength to carry on his legacy from here on in. I love you Drew.

My Weak Generation

I would not be the only person to ever feel that they don't belong in their current generation. I just look at my peers and I wonder how the hell we grew up in the same time. I'm extremely old- fashioned, this has to do with old-fashioned parents of ethnic descent. I still believe in chivalry, despite the feminist movement killing it. I can't help it though, if a seat opens up on the subway and I see a woman standing, I wait to see if she'll sit down before I take the seat. It angers me when a guy around my age takes it but that is a seldom occurrence so there may be hope just yet. The problem with my generation is that nothing shocks us. We give people a pass way too often. I get to see this in its most blatant form because I am an avid fan of professional wrestling. People will say whatever they want about pro wrestling and the wrestlers, but consistently it is the highest rated show. More people go to WWEUniverse.com than twitter, Facebook or Myspace and Monday Night Raw is the longest episodic TV show in history for a reason at over 800 episodes. Given these statistics, I know that there are a lot of closet fans because most people say they don't watch professional wrestling. I guess I'll form my criticisms with our generation through WWE first, then branch off into more general criticisms.

In the WWE, there are faces and heels. Heels are people who say and do things so that the people will boo them. Read any wrestler's book, they will tell you that they like being a heel more than a face (the wrestlers that people like). Now there is nothing wrong with this set up in and of itself. Obviously since the athletes will do battle, (granted scripted but fans put that aside) they want it to be good vs. evil. The problem I have that is indicative of our generation is how fluidly and easily heels become faces and faces become heels.

Triple H is one of the best heels of all time, but then all he has to do is do some crotch chops and yell "Degeneration X" and all is forgiven and he is cheered. Before that, Triple H comes out again and again insulting the city that the event is currently in, cheating to win, lying, showing himself to be a horrible human being, and in one swoop motion, all the previous atrocities are forgotten. It's not just with Triple H, every wrestler does the same thing. I can't think of one wrestler that stayed a face or a heel throughout their entire career. For me, no matter what angle Vince McMahon thinks up, I have never and will never boo the Undertaker. He will never be a heel for me. Even Hulk Hogan and Stone Cold Steve Austin have turned heel. Stone Cold is most unique because the whole beer drinking, middle finger raising, bad ass persona was designed to be a heel, but people loved it. Some may take this to mean our generation defies authority and sticks it to the man, but we really don't. Instead, we're afraid to act, timid and incapable of standing up for what we believe in. People cheered Steve Austin because he was doing what they wanted to do, not what they would ever do. What did it take for Steve Austin to become heel? He became friends with Vince McMahon and wore a suit. It was that easy. Even Vince McMahon turns from face to heel effortlessly and that's usually the way to get someone to become a heel. By joining Vince McMahon and being a corporate guy, he says one nice thing about a city and all the negative things he's said goes out the window. My generation has absolutely no memory.

I include people's reactions to heels to emphasize the broader point that we do not hold people accountable for their words and actions. Sure we condemn it and give lip service to how we don't like it, but we do nothing. The lead singer of the Fugees Lauryn Hill said on MTV, "I'd rather see a Black kid starve than a White person buy my CD."

If White people had any decency or self-respect, they would boycott her CD. Instead, White people still bought it. Now, I never bought a

Fugees CD, and even if she hadn't said it I wouldn't because I'm not a very big fan of their music. I definitely wasn't going to buy a CD after she said that.

Similarly, and more recently, Kanye West had yet another disrespectful moment when he interrupted 19-year-old country singer Taylor Swift at the 2009 VMA's. He's had a lot of incidents, to the point that *Southpark* did an episode to make fun of him called "Fish Sticks." Basically, he goes around telling everyone he's a genius and is offended that everyone calls him a "Gay Fish."

They get this from a joke that becomes popular in which you ask a male, "Do you like Fish Sticks" and they say, "Yes." You may or may not follow with, "Do you like putting Fish Sticks in your mouth?" They say, "Yes" again, then you say, "Wow, what are you a Gay Fish?"

In the show Kanye West is the only person not to get the joke and even kills someone for calling him a Gay Fish because you can't insult an entrepreneurial word-smith genius like him. The episode happened before the VMA's, but naturally they advertised it on their web site afterwards. I will not support Kanye West any more for this. He can blame alcohol and apologize all he wants but I don't accept apologies when you continually do things like this. I know nobody in my generation will follow. I originally thought the phrase, "No press is bad press" was false. When I see how there are absolutely no financial or otherwise consequences to celebrity actions, I disagree. Terrell Owens continually finds teams to play for even though he wrecks every team he goes to.

I can't think of one instance in our generation where we boycotted anything. The closest thing I can come to is Papa John's sold "Crybaby"shirts to mock LeBron James, when the Washington Wizards called him that. Clevelanders immediately boycotted Papa John's Pizza. Even when Papa John's apologized, Cleveland didn't let up. It was only when Papa John's started selling slices of pizza in Cleveland for a quarter as a sign of apology to the city of Cleveland, did Clevelanders lift their boycott. I commend Clevelanders for supporting LeBron James and sticking to their guns. By the way LeBron, New York will not do this for you, think about that before you decide to leave. I wonder what my favorite NBA team is.

Although I do not agree with the hippy movement, at least they were taking a stand against something. The lock-ins and Woodstock meant something. The Woodstock that happened 10 years ago was just so they could party. There are protests now, but protests don't impress me, boycotts do. Sacrificing something you enjoy to make a point, that shows commitment.

In closing, I would encourage you to form a set of beliefs and stand by them in the face of controversy. The 2004 campaign vilified the word "flip-flop" and rightly so. This doesn't mean you can't change your mind about an issue. Engage in debates with people who don't agree with you, see if there's any logic to what they're saying and try to keep an open mind. If someone convinces you, then you can change your mind. If you have a reason why you flip-flopped, then it's okay but don't be afraid to speak your mind. We cannot be in fear of making a mistake. I've said a lot of dumb things and people will strike me down for them and it makes me smarter and you learn from it and move on. Now, everyone is always looking around asking for permission to say things. This country gave you freedom of speech, use it.

Now, it would be ironic if people boycott this book because of its controversial views. I guess it would be a step in the right direction, but obviously, I wouldn't be too happy about it.

BIBLIOGRAPHY

1. Gregory, Andre, and Wallace Shawn. "Dinner with Andre." *Dinner with Andre.* Saga Productions. 11 Oct.. 1981.Movie.

2. Sedaris, David. Me Talk Pretty One Day. New York: Little Brown and CO., 2000. Print

3. Sorba, Ryan. *The Truth is Finally Coming Out of the Closet.* TS.

4. Aristotle. Poetics. New York: The Penquin Group, 1996. Print

5. Plato, and Alexander Kerr. *The Republic.* Chicago: Charles Kerr & CO., 1915. Print.

6. Rand, Ayn, and Leonard Peikoff. *Fountainhead.* New York: New American Library, 1943. Print.

7. Rand, Ayn. Atlas Shrugged. New York: Penquin Group, 1957. Print

8. Woods, Thomas E. *The Politically Incorrect Guide to American History.* Washington D.C.: Regnery, 2004. Print.

9. Levitt, Stephen D., and Stephen J. Dubner. *Freakonomics.* New York: HarperCollins, 2005. Print.

10. Gladwell, Malcolm. *Blink: The Power of Thinking Withough Thinking.* New York: Little Brown & Company, 2005. Print.

11. *Abortion TV.* Fear Media Inc. Web. 3 Dec. 2009. <http://www.abortiontv.com/Misc/AbortionStatistics.htm#United%20States>.

12. Montaldo, Charles. "About.co." State by State Juvenile Arrest Rates. New York Times Company, 2009. Web. 3 Dec. 2009. <http://crime.about.com/od/stats/a/rates_juvenile.htm>.13. State of Fear

15. *Avenue Q.* By Robert Lopez and Jeff Marx. 340 West 50th Street, New York. 21 Mar. 2006. Performance.

16. Rock, Chris. "Chris Rock: Bigger and BLacker." *Chris Rock Bigger and Blacker.* HBO. New York, New York, 10 July 1999. Television.

17. Rock, Chris. "Chris Rock: Never Scared." *Chris Rock: Never Scared.* Dir. Joel Gallen. HBO. New York, New York, 17 Apr. 2004. Television.

19. *Southpark STudios.com.* Web. 11 Dec. 2009. <http://www.southparkstudios.com/>.

20. *The O'Reilly Factor.* Fox. Bristol, CT. Television.

21. Dan, Brown. Angels and Demons. New York: PocketBooks, NY. Print

22. Kraukaur, Jon. *Under the Banenr of Heaven.* New York: Random House Inc., NY. Print.

24. *Fight Club.* Dir. David Fincher. Perf. Brad Pitt Edward Norton. Fox 2000 Pictures, 1999. Film.

25. *The Rasmus News.* Rasmus, 18 Nov. 2009. Web. 18 Nov. 2009.

26. *The best of Chris Farley.* Perf. Chris Farley. SNL, 2003. DVD.

27. *Louis C.K Shameless.* Perf. Louis C.K. HBO, 2007. DVD.

28. Edmonds, Rosemary. *War and Peace.* New York: Penquin Books, 1982. Print.

29. Anonymous. *The Jewish Peril Protocals of the Learned Elders of Zion.* Kessinger, 2004. Print.

30. Coulter, Ann. *Guilty.* Three Rivers PR, 2009. Print.

31. Castiglione, Baldassarre. *The Book of the Courtier*. England: Penquin Books, 1967. Print.

32. Darwin, Charles. *The Origin of Species: 150th Anniversary Edition*. New York: Barnes and Noble Classics Series. Print.

33. Darwin, Charles. *The Origin of Species: 150th Anniversary Edition*. New York: Barnes and Noble Classics Series. Print.

34. *George Carlin: You are all diseased*. Perf. George Carlin. HBO, 2003. DVD.

35. Rand, Ayn. *We the Living*. Signet, 1996. Print.

36. "Front Page." *La Repubblica* [Florence, Italy] 2 Feb. 2004. Print.

37. *Dave Chappelle Killing the Softly*. Perf. Dave Chappelle. Platinum Comedy Series, 2000. DVD.

39. *Ethnic Slurs.com*. Web. 18 Dec. 2009. <http://www.ethnicslurs.com>.

41. *Do the Right Thing*. Dir. Spike Lee. Spike Lee, 1989. DVD.

42. *Coach Carter*. Dir. Samuel L. Jackson. Paramount Pictures, 2005. DVD.

43. *Coach Carter*. Dir. Samuel L. Jackson. Paramount Pictures, 2005. DVD.

44. Carson, Rachel. *Silent Spring*. Boston: Houghton Mifflin, 1962. Print.

45. *EuroTrip*. Dir. Jeff Schafer. Perf. Scott Mechlowicz, Jacob Pitts,Michelle Trachenberg, Travis Wester. Freebase, 2004. DVD.

46. *The Plain Dealer* [Cleveland] 12 Sept. 2001: 1-1. Print.

47. *Www.Nielson.com*. Nielson Research Media. Web. 24 Dec. 2009.

www.ingramcontent.com/pod-product-compliance
Lightning Source LLC
Chambersburg PA
CBHW020418290526
45785CB00002B/625